D1199054

The German-Russians

The German-Russians

A Bibliography
of Russian Materials with Introductory
Essay, Annotations, and Locations of Materials
in Major American and Soviet Libraries

James Long

Clio Books

Santa Barbara, California
Oxford, England

Library of Congress Cataloging in Publication Data
Long, James W., 1942–
    The German-Russians.

    Includes indexes.
    1. Germans in Russia—History—Bibliography.
I. Title.
Z2517.G4L65   [DK34.G3]   016.947′004′31
ISBN 0-87436-282-2   78-19071

American Bibliographical Center—Clio Press
2040 Alameda Padre Serra
Santa Barbara, California 93103

        Clio Press, Ltd.
Woodside House, Hinksey Hill
Oxford OX1 5BE, England

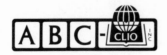

Manufactured in the United States of America

First printing, 1979
1   2   3   4   5   6   7   8   9

For
Pat

Contents

Preface

This bibliography lists and annotates books, pamphlets, and articles in Russian dealing with the German-Russians. The German-Russians comprise a unique ethnic group which consisted primarily of German-speaking peoples, who immigrated to Russia in the eighteenth and nineteenth centuries and settled in colonies mainly in the Lower Volga and in southern Russia along the Black Sea littoral. Tsarist and Soviet policies led to subsequent migrations of the descendants of these colonists to the West and other parts of the Russian and Soviet empires. Today German-Russians are living in places as widely scattered as Soviet Central Asia, West Germany, Canada, the United States, and South America. In the United States tens of thousands of them moved into the Dakotas, Kansas, Nebraska, Colorado, California, and Washington.

The unusual history and frequent wanderings of these former colonists have generated considerable interest in and prodigious research on the German-Russians in Western Europe, the United States, and South America. Two events chiefly account for the current interest in the German-Russians. The first was the exodus of a significant number of them from Russia, primarily during the 1880-1920 period. As a result, the desire by many Americans to rediscover and preserve the memory of their origins has resulted in thousands of German-Russian immigrant families delving into the history of their forefathers to discover their ethnic roots. The American Historical Society of Germans from Russia and the North Dakota Historical Society of Germans from Russia were both organized to facilitate this quest for the preservation of the German-Russian heritage. The second event, which so tragically brought the German-Russians to world attention, was Stalin's wholesale and ruthless deportation of the German-Russians to Central Asia during World War II. Since Stalin's death the German-Russians have repeatedly petitioned and even demonstrated to obtain permission to return to their original settlements in

Russia or to emigrate. In 1976 alone, 9,600 ethnic Germans emigrated from the Soviet Union to West Germany.

Almost all research on the German-Russians has been based on German sources, many of which are preserved in the *Landsmannschaft der Deutschen aus Russland* and the *Institut für Auslandsbeziehungen* in West Germany. Dr. Karl Stumpp has published an extensive German-language bibliography of German-Russian literature entitled *Das Schrifttum über das Deutschtum in Russland*. Few scholars have endeavored to use Russian materials. Utilization of the rich Russian materials will contribute greatly to a fuller understanding of the history of the German-Russians. The purpose of this bibliography is to facilitate research by scholars and students and to provide an insight into a most interesting ethnic group.

Acknowledgments

Space considerations preclude listing the many persons who have provided helpful advice and counsel during the preparation of this work. I owe a special debt of gratitude to two individuals for sharing constantly their encyclopedic bibliographic knowledge: Dr. Robert V. Allen, Russia and Soviet Union area specialist in the Slavic and Central European Division of the Library of Congress, and Dr. David G. Rempel, professor emeritus of the College of San Mateo. To Mrs. Arlene Paul and the Hoover Institution staff and to Dr. Victor Koressaar and his New York Public Library Slavonic Division staff I extend my thanks for so willingly and unquestioningly searching for some obscure items. I greatly appreciated the assistance of William Virden during the initial stages of preparing this bibliography. Above all others, I wish to thank Pat, Marc, and David for their patience and understanding during the six-month separation while I was in the Soviet Union conducting research.

Financial assistance from Colorado State University, the Germans from Russia in Colorado Study Project, and the International Research and Exchanges Board made this study possible and is gratefully acknowledged.

I wish to make special acknowledgments to St. Martin's Press, Inc. and Macmillan & Co., Ltd. for permission to quote from Alexander Dallin, *German Rule in Russia 1941–1945. A Study of Occupation Policies* and to Colorado State University for permission to quote from my preliminary study *Russian Language Sources Relating to the Germans from Russia*.

All errors of omission and commission herein are my own. Finally, all corrections and comments from those who use this bibliography will be gratefully welcomed.

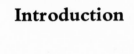

Introduction

Introduction

Tsarist autocracy and Soviet totalitarianism, both of which in varying degrees controlled public expression, naturally influenced the direction and extent of research and publication of materials on the former German colonies in Russia. The study of the German colonists invariably was affected by erratic government policies, which alternated between the extremes of granting national autonomy and enforcing russification of nationalities. To place Russian historical research and the availability of Russian language sources in their proper historical context, this Introduction is divided into four parts. The first section is a general survey of tsarist and Soviet policies and attitudes vis-à-vis the Germans in Russia. The second section is a more detailed discussion of Russian primary sources pertinent to the German experience; the third section covers Russian and Soviet research on the Germans in Russia; and the fourth section explains the format of this bibliography.

The Germans in Russia and the Soviet Union

The large-scale settlement of foreign peoples in Russia directed by the tsarist government occurred in two major waves. The earliest, during the third quarter of the eighteenth century, resulted from the 22 July 1763 manifesto of Catherine II and the unsettled economic situation in western Europe following the disruptive Seven Years' War. Catherine's manifesto promised to all foreigners who settled permanently as agriculturalists in Russia freedom of religion, noninterference by government bureaucrats in the internal administration of each colony, thirty years' exemption from taxation and government services, exemption from military service, with volunteers granted a thirty-ruble bonus, and interest-free government loans to purchase livestock and equipment, with repayment due only ten years after receipt of the loan. Areas of potential colonization mentioned in the manifesto included western Siberia and the provinces of Astrakhan, Orenburg, and Voronezh, with the foreign immigrants being supervised and settled by a specifically established institution, the *Kantseliariia opekunstva inostrannykh poselentsev* [Chancellery for the Guardianship of Foreign Settlers].[1] Between 1764 and 1773, tsarist agents and private recruiters directed 23, 504 foreign colonists to the Lower Volga and founded 104 settlements on both sides of the Volga near the city of Saratov, with the largest number of settlers arriving between 1764 and 1766.[2] The overwhelming majority of the Volga settlers were German-speaking Evangelicals from Hesse and the Rhinelands.[3] The first Russo-Turkish war (1768–1774) and Pugachev's rebellion (1773–1774) diverted the government's attention from its colonization program and ended the first period of foreign settlement in Russia.

On 20 February 1804 Alexander I (1801–1825) issued a manifesto again inviting foreigners to settle in Russia, which initiated the second wave of foreign settlement needed to populate the vast, recently acquired lands of the Black Sea littoral called New Russia.[4] Russia's acquisition of Bessarabia in 1812 added even more new territory for settlement, and caused this second period of foreign immigration to continue until the 1820s. The devastation wreaked on western Europe during the Napoleonic wars made Alexander's invitation very alluring. The 1804 manifesto generally followed the major lines of the 1763 manifesto, but there were significant changes incorporated to insure that only "model agriculturalists" with advanced agricultural techniques and financial security would settle on Russian lands, and to restrict the flow of foreigners to two hundred families each year.[5] Exemptions from taxation and other government obligations were reduced to ten years; each family, regardless of size, could receive up to 216 acres (80 dessiatines) of land upon agreement to pay between fifteen and twenty copecks per dessiatine after ten years; finally, each family had to be solvent and possess at least 300 gulden in currency or property, and be of sound moral character. The second group of immigrants was much more heterogeneous than the first. German-speaking peoples from south and southwest Germany (Baden, Alsace, Württemberg, The Palatinate, and Hesse) comprised a large part of the new settlers, but there were also significant numbers of Greeks, Bulgarians, Armenians, and Albanians. Although Evangelicals comprised the largest religious group of the German-speaking Black Sea colonies, the Catholics and Mennonites were well represented.

Russian documents and records referred to the Volga and Black Sea Germans as simply *nemetskie kolonisty* [German colonists], which concealed their quite different experiences in Russia. The tsarist government clearly distinguished the German colonists from the Baltic Germans, who were "annexed" rather than settled by the Russian government early in the eighteenth century, and from the Mennonites, who spoke Dutch or German but had very different life-styles and religious beliefs.

The similar religious and cultural traditions brought by the Volga and Black Sea Germans from Germany provided a certain common bond, but their quite varied experiences in Russia increasingly differentiated the two groups. The Volga Germans' avowed purpose was primarily to act as homesteaders on Russia's rugged, semiarid southeastern frontier and as a buffer against marauding Asiatic nomads, whereas the Black Sea Germans were to serve primarily as model farmers for the neighboring Great and Little Russians by tilling the rich, black-soil steppe of New Russia. The Volga Germans quickly adopted communal landholding in the form of the Russian *obshchina* or *mir* system, which normally resulted in periodic redistributions of the land to equalize household landholdings. The Black Sea Germans adopted a form of entailed estate whereby the family's holdings were usually passed on undivided to the youngest son. As a result, Black Sea German families resorted to the purchase of additional lands for the elder sons from the readily available state and private estate lands. The Volga Germans could not easily lease or purchase large amounts of additional lands because of the paucity of large, private estates in this frontier region and the unavailability of state lands. Finally, the Black Sea settlements were much more geographically dispersed and had greater contact and visibility with non-German settlements. This greater visibility, as well as the prosperity of their farms, made the Black Sea Germans the object of vitriolic Ukrainian and Russian nationalist attacks beginning in the last quarter of the nineteenth century, while the densely settled and less prosperous Volga colonies remained much more isolated from the Slavic population.[6] Notwithstanding the government's attitude of viewing the German-speaking settlers (except the Mennonites) as a relatively homogeneous group, the two areas of settlement developed quite differently.

The German-speaking colonists remained relative strangers in the Russian empire primarily because government policy generally fostered their physical and cultural isolation, and the Germans brought with them strong historical and cultural traditions. Not until the last years of the tsarist empire was there a concerted effort to assimilate forcibly the numerous nationalities residing within the Russian state. For over a century, the Germans freely perpetuated a western European past by memorizing Protestant and Catholic catechisms, reciting German folktales, speaking their native language with its unique historical connotations, and living according to German customs and folkways. The tsar's government could not quickly eradicate the German traditions, which had been lived, learned, and popularized for centuries. Similarly, the *mir* system and growing land scarcity not only generally precluded intercolony population shifts, but also prevented the intrusion of non-Germans into the colonial towns and villages. Even the Stalinist totalitarian state failed to obliterate German traditions by removing the Germans from their historic lands and scattering them to remote areas of the Soviet Union.

For over a hundred years the German colonists enjoyed highly preferential treatment in Russia resulting from the generous concessions granted the original settlers. The Russian government provided tax exemptions from five to ten, and in some cases thirty, years; exemption from military service; freedom of worship; loans and subsidies that were partially or entirely free of interest; and a large measure of autonomy within the settlements. Most settlements established schools, and these German schools suffered relatively little government interference. Compared to Russian peasants, each immigrant family received generous land allotments, with empty reserve lands set aside to accommodate the anticipated natural increase of settlers.

Farming became the vocation of the Germans in Russia. The original purpose of the recruitment of foreign colonists was to have them develop the vast new lands acquired in the south and east of European Russia. There was also strong interest in the colonists as a civilizing force for the Russian peasants. Tsarist officials hoped the colonists' example would transform the Russian peasant into a thrifty and practical *Bauer* [farmer]. In April 1846, the Ministry of State Domains inaugurated the monthly publication of the *Unterhaltungsblatt für deutsche Ansiedler im südlichen Russland* to acquaint colonists with agricultural improvements, which would "serve to develop the colonists' curiosity and spirit of industriousness."[7] The Black Sea German system of landholding and farming was even extolled as the one best suited for adoption by the emancipated Russian serfs.[8]

As a result of Russia's humiliating defeat in the Crimean War and growing peasant unrest in Russia, Emperor Alexander II (1855–1881) embarked upon a broad program of reform intended to modernize Russia while preserving autocracy. The reform significantly altered the lives of the Germans by abolishing many of their privileges and integrating them more into Russian administration and supervision. *Zemstvos*, institutions of rural self-government, intruded upon local autonomy. One of the *zemstvo* functions was the construction and administration of schools, and by the late 1860s, *zemstvo* officials began to assume greater control over the German schools.[9] In 1871 the colonies were placed directly under the control of Russian provincial and district authorities, and the Chancellery for the Guardianship of Foreign Settlers was abolished. Although not always immediately and favorably responsive, this special office had at least assured the colonists that their petitions were heard. In 1874 Minister of Defense Dmitrii Miliutin announced universal military conscription, which introduced the democratic concept of the obligation of all classes to serve. Although not all eligible German males would have had to serve, the revocation of exemption from military service so alarmed the colonists that some decided to emigrate from Russia.[10]

The Germans in Russia barely had time to adjust to the loss of their privileges when a wave of extreme russification began to sweep the country. It id not ebb until the fall of the tsarist regime in 1917. After the assassination of Alexander II in 1881, the dominant groups in the ruling class encouraged an uncompromising application of the principles of autocracy, orthodoxy, and russification to save the country from the revolutionary events sweeping through the Russian empire. The intolerance, chauvinism, and repression that characterized official russification had a great deal of popular support. Many Russians believed that the growing nationalism in the border areas populated by Ukrainians, Poles, Baltic peoples, and Finns would lead to separation from Russia, and they were willing to see steps taken to prevent the disintegration of the Russian empire. Consequently, all nationalities suffered under this growing suspicion.

The physical and cultural isolation of the Germans in Russia became a target for attack. Numerous Russian authors took up the assimilation banner and wrote polemics directed at the Germans' aloofness from the rest of Russian society. In 1897 all German schools were subordinated to the Ministry of Education, and Russian language instruction became mandatory.[11] The growing anti-German feeling became especially virulent during World War I and culminated in the government's expropriation and confiscation of the settlers' lands.[12] Fortunately for most of the colonists, the revolutions of 1917 intervened to impede the full implementation of the wartime land legislation.

The weakness of the Bolshevik government caused by the dislocation and destruction of World War I and the Civil War (1918–1921) resulted in a relatively lenient attitude towards the Volga Germans in the 1920s. In 1924 the Volga Germans were favored by being the first granted status of an autonomous republic in the territory of the Lower Volga region. The German Volga Autonomous Soviet Socialist Republic [*Nemtsev Povolzh'ia Avtonomnaia Sovetskaia Sotsialischeskaia Respublika*] survived until 1941. During this period, the use of the German language was encouraged and seminal work in the study of the German dialects began.

Beginning in the 1930s the Germans in Russia again experienced harsh times. Stalin's "second revolution," which envisaged the rapid transformation of the USSR into a fully socialist state by means of the rapid collectivization of the countryside, especially affected the predominantly rural Germans. Blotting out the documentation of brutal excesses of collectivization by Stalin and his successors has left a serious gap in the recorded history of the Germans in Russia.

This historical gap turned into a void when the Germans became part of the "Gulag Archipelago," Stalin's all-pervasive structure of forced-labor camps. The massive deportation of Germans began after Hitler's invasion on 22 June 1941. Aleksandr Solzhenitsyn claims that the Volga German territory formed a unique part of the Archipelago.[13] Very little is known about the execution of the German diaspora. The Germans disappeared from the face of the Soviet earth and even from books. In 1939 Soviet authorities devoted five pages in the *Great Soviet Encyclopedia* to the Volga Germans; by 1950, when the next edition appeared, the Volga Germans had been conspicuously expurgated.[14] Uncorroborated reports in the 1940s of the relocation of the Germans to remote parts of the Soviet empire provided the only hint of the continued survival of the Germans in Russia.

Although subject to the same forced evacuation decree as the Volga Germans, the *Volksdeutsche*, or ethnic Germans in the Black Sea area, largely escaped Soviet liquidation because of the rapid advance of German forces into southern Russia. German occupation authorities granted the Black Sea German communities highly preferential treatment, even though their role in the future order of the Third Reich was unclear. Alexander Dallin, the foremost authority on the subject, wrote:

> The advantages of the Volksdeutsche, though varying from area to area, were significant enough for the rest of the people to view them as the most privileged group—so much so that some non-Germans sought to demonstrate the existence of an imaginary "German grandmother" in order to share in the privileges.[15]

Fearful of Soviet retaliation for alleged or actual collaboration, about 300,000 of the Black Sea Germans abandoned their homes and fled the Soviet Union with the retreating German troops.

In 1956 the history of the nationalities suppressed during World War II began to unfold. In his secret report to the Twentieth Party Congress, First Party Secretary Nikita Khrushchev denounced Stalin's forced deportation of the Moslem Karachais, Chechens, Ingushi, Balkars, and the Buddhist Kalmyks. These five nationalities were allowed to return to their original homes. Khrushchev notably omitted any reference to the deported Germans and Crimean Tatars.

Since 1964 the Party has pursued a partial, inconsistent rehabilitation of the Soviet Germans. In its decree of 29 August 1964, the Presidium of the USSR Supreme Soviet stated that the previous blanket accusations leveled at the Soviet Germans had been unfounded, a manifestation of arbitrariness that was an outcome of the Stalin personality cult. The decree did not provide for the resettlement of the Germans in their original homes, ostensibly because the regions of their prewar domicile had already become occupied by other Soviet citizens. Soviet leaders justify this dualistic resettlement policy by claiming that the five resettled nationalities have returned to vacant, unoccupied lands, while the resettlement of the Germans and Tatars would necessitate the relocation of large numbers of people. It seems that the real reason the Germans have not been granted permission to return to their original homes is that Soviet authorities consider them essential for the continued economic development of those regions where they are now living.[16]

The 1964 "pardon" has entitled the Soviet Germans to the slight degree of cultural autonomy enjoyed by other nationalities in the Soviet Union. They now have their own weekly newspaper, *Neues Leben*.[17] Like all Soviet newspapers, it is highly propagandistic, yet it keeps alive German culture. It is published in German and contains articles on Soviet German folkways, writers, and artists. Local publishing houses publish works by Soviet German authors and other literature for German speakers. Some Soviet Germans are being allowed to immigrate to the West; however, they are still not permitted to return to their original Soviet homes despite the Party's claim that Soviet Germans are free to choose where to live in the USSR. A few relatives of former German residents of Russia have been allowed to visit with relatives still living in the Soviet Union. Most recently, some Soviet Germans have become actively involved in the nascent human rights movement.[18]

Because it is not part of the history curriculum in schools, the history of the German settlers is relatively unknown among the Soviet populace. In a new Soviet textbook for university students, "foreign colonists" [*inostrannye kolonisty*] are mentioned in a chart as one of the privileged groups in eighteenth-century Russia, along with the nobility, clergy, and merchantry.[19] Unlike the other privileged groups listed, no mention is made of the "foreign colonists" in the text of the book. The Volga German settlers are completely omitted in the same textbook's two-page section "Peoples of the Volga" [*Narody Povolzh'ia*].[20] The history of the German colonists is still not considered a proper subject for Soviet university students.[21]

Historical distortion also still permeates the literature written for foreigners. A good example is the recently published booklet, *Papa Dell and His Family–The Life of Soviet Citizens of German Origin*, which is freely and readily available at airports, hotels, and train stations. Four sentences describe the settlers' life and history in the eighteenth and nineteenth centuries. German settlers are depicted as Marxian revolutionaries who immediately flocked to the Bolsheviks after the November 1917 revolution. Finally, the book reiterates the lie of the forced deportation of the Germans during World War II:

> Nazi Germans' treacherous invasion of the USSR was a grim test for all the Soviet peoples, including the Soviet Germans. In 1941 it became imperative to organize the wholesale evacuation of the population from regions directly menaced by Nazi

occupation. The Volga Germans were evacuated to trans-Urals areas. . . . The torrent
of Nazi wartime anti-Soviet propaganda and unremitting calls to those known as
'Volksdeutsche' were in some measure responsible for Soviet Germans becoming
suspect in the complex situation of war.[22]

For over two centuries the descendants of the first German colonists
have preserved their ethnic identity. They have continued, if unwillingly,
their eastward migration, populating and developing the Russian and
Soviet frontiers like their forefathers. They have stoically persevered
under absolutist regimes, including one which brutally tried to blot them
from history. As their official designation, "Soviet Germans," suggests,
they are Soviet citizens, but ethnically most of them remain German. They
have precariously survived but still remain strangers in a strange land.

Russian Primary Sources

Russian primary sources on the Germans in Russia are abundant but not
always easily accessible to scholars. The term "primary source" here
means the first recording of an event or eyewitness accounts, such as
institutional records, memoirs, letters, and newspapers, which are used by
researchers to produce secondary accounts. Section three of this Introduction covers Russian research and publication of secondary sources relating
to the Germans in Russia.

Generally, Russian primary sources are official government publications describing and quantifying the economic development of the German colonies. These publications reached their greatest magnitude during
the last four decades of the tsarist epoch. Until the 1860s, the predominantly state-owned and -controlled Russian press published general and
official accounts of the *nemetskie kolonisty*, the government appellation for
the German settlers. With the proliferation of publications by organs of
local self-government in the 1860s, publications for the first time began to
narrate the conditions found in local German settlements. The physical
and cultural isolation of the Germans from the Slavic population is
reflected in the paucity of primary sources which depict the settlers' social
structure and mores.

No attempt has been made here to provide comprehensive coverage
of Russian archival materials because the sensitive nature of the topic still
precludes extensive archival research by scholars. Published guides indi-
cate the richness of archival materials, but the capriciousness of archival
administrators makes access very precarious.[23] The Central State Historical Archive of the USSR (TsGIA) houses most materials relating to the
German experience under tsarist rule (1763–1917). The records of the
Ministry of State Domains as well as the Department of Religious Affairs
and Foreign Confessions are in TsGIA. The Leningrad-based archive's

working conditions and staff are easily among the best the Soviet Union has to offer, and recently some western scholars have been granted permission to investigate specifically defined topics tangential to the German experience in Russia.

Provided they survived the ravages of nature and two world wars, the records of township executive boards [*volostnye pravleniia*] could open up a rich, new fund of information on the German colonies. After 1861, the *volost*, or township, a territorial-administrative subdivision consisting of one or several villages, enjoyed some degree of self-government. In 1913 the Saratov Archival Commission discovered that some townships in Saratov Province had initiated record-keeping much earlier than the 1860s:

> This is often especially found in the townships composed of villages of former state peasants, and above all, in the townships of the German colonists. The oldest records in these [townships] date back to the last quarter of the eighteenth century. . . . In the colonists' townships there are archives containing more than 10,000 files and books. . . . [24]

Though the Soviets have allowed foreigners access to the central state archives, prospects seem remote that the *volost* records will be utilized by foreign scholars in the near future.

The legal status of the German colonists is documented in the Complete Collection of Laws [*Polnoe Sobranie Zakonov*], hereafter referred to as *PSZ*. There are three editions of the *PSZ* covering the period 1649–1913, which include the complete texts of laws. The *PSZ* is arranged chronologically, but all three editions have indexes which contain specific references to the legislation regulating the status of the German colonists. For example, the first edition contains the official manifesto granted by Catherine II to the colonists on 22 July 1763.[25] Unfortunately, the *PSZ* contains only the final laws as enacted and not the drafts used in the formulation of those laws.

Beginning in 1837 the Ministry of State Domains assumed administrative jurisdiction over the state peasants and all other groups living on state lands, replacing the Ministry of the Interior which had supervised the colonies between 1802 and 1837. Between 1840 and 1860, the Ministry of State Domains published several official accounts of the foreign settlers in the *Zhurnal ministerstva gosudarstvennykh imushchestv*. The focus of these articles was on the settlement and economic development of the foreign colonies. They are particularly rich in demographic statistics and provide valuable insights into the agricultural innovations and problems of the Germans.[26] The Ministry of the Interior also published articles of this same type, but fewer in number, in its official journal, *Zhurnal ministerstva vnutrennikh del*. Unfortunately, this narrow official focus on the colonists as agriculturalists and producers left little printed space for the societal structure and folkways of the Germans.

Until the emancipation of the serfs in 1861, the only major population

survey was the ten revisions, or censuses, of the people subject to the poll
tax [*podushnoe oblozhenie*]. This meant primarily the serfs, because the
nobility, clergy, Cossacks, and other privileged groups did not have to
pay the poll tax. Although originally exempted from the poll tax for thirty
years, the colonists were enumerated in the last six revisions, which took
place in 1795, 1811, 1815, 1833, 1850, and 1857–58. Despite the inac-
curacies of data, poor administrative implementation, and lack of comprehensiveness, the revisions did provide age, name and place of birth of
males, permanent residence, distribution by sex, and amount of taxes paid
to the treasury. Unfortunately, published revision materials are rare, and
the original revision reports remain in Soviet archives.[27]

Postemancipation population statistics greatly improved in accuracy
and standardization of reporting with the establishment of the Central
Statistical Committee in the Ministry of the Interior under the able
directorship of the prominent geographer, Petr Petrovich Semenov-
Tian-Shanskii. Between 1861 and 1885, the committee published various
provincial population reports. Each province had a volume which contained an introductory chapter on the people, land, and economy; a main
body of demographic information; and an appendix of provincial maps.
Statistical data on the colonies provided information on the number of
households, distribution by sex, and churches, schools, and local enter-
prises (dairies, flour mills, tanneries, etc.).[28] The results of the Central
Statistical Committee investigations revealed the need for a comprehensive survey of the Russian empire.

In 1874 a general census became mandatory for the successful and
equitable implementation of universal military conscription. However,
government indecision, bureaucratic infighting, and interminable discus-
sions delayed administrative execution for twenty-three years. Finally, in
1897 the tsarist government conducted its first and last general census of
the Russian empire.[29] The Central Statistical Committee administered
data collection, compiled the results, and published its findings in 89
volumes under the general title *Pervaia vseobshchaia perepis' naseleniia rossiiskoi imperii, 1897 g*. Each province was allotted at least one volume, with
the larger provinces requiring two or three. The comprehensiveness and
greater reliability of the demographic data make the 1897 census a valuable
resource tool for the study of the Germans in Russia.

Undoubtedly, the most valuable source materials pertaining to the
German settlers during the last five decades of the tsarist regime were the
zemstvo publications. In 1864 Tsar Alexander II ordered the establishment
of *zemstvos* in most parts of the Russian empire to deal primarily with local
economic needs. These institutions were created at the district and provincial levels. The *zemstvos* provided valuable social services to the peoples of
Russia and bequeathed to historians invaluable materials on provincial and

local life. The most prolific period of *zemstvo* publishing was from 1890 to 1905; although publications never ceased, they only appeared irregularly during the revolutionary years 1905–1908 and during World War I.[30]

The multitude of *zemstvo* publications shed much-needed light on rural life in Russia. In the 1880s and 1890s most provincial *zemstvos* published very useful collections of statistics.[31] District *zemstvos* regularly collected economic and demographic information, such as population, acreage farmed, harvests, and livestock holdings. It is possible by utilizing these materials to draw comparisons between the life of the Russian peasant and the German farmer. *Zemstvo* doctors reported and discussed the prevalence of trachoma and tuberculosis of the bone among the German settlers; education inspectors observed German church-parish schools and encouraged the creation of cooperative schools among German families.[32] *Zemstvo* statisticians documented a phenomenal population explosion in the Volga German settlements. Virtually all aspects of the settlers' lives were touched upon in *zemstvo* publications.

Russian records provide little information to the researcher studying German emigration from Russia, which accelerated after 1875. A Soviet authority on Russian emigration remarked that investigators of Russian emigration must rely on the immigration records of those countries receiving the Russian emigrant or the records of foreign exit ports, particularly German and English ports from which most Russian citizens departed.[33] Under the tsarist regime a Russian citizen had the legal right neither to reside permanently in a foreign country nor to become a citizen of a foreign country. According to Russian law, Russian citizens could visit or live abroad for periods up to five years. After that time, if the applicant had not petitioned for an extended grace period of residence abroad from the provincial governor's office where the passport was issued, the subject was considered to have broken the law by fleeing Russia. Consequently, most Russian emigration statistics are simply exit and entrance figures of individuals allegedly leaving the country for short periods. Information about age, nationality, family composition, occupation, and country of destination is absent. Bureaucratic hassles and the illegality of permanent emigration forced many Russian citizens to flee the country illegally.[34]

Soviet primary sources on the Germans in Russia no doubt exist in large numbers, but most are inaccessible to the scholar and the remainder are of dubious value. The turbulent revolutionary and civil war years, the scarcity of paper in the 1920s, and the excesses of the Stalinist regime in the 1930s all took their toll. The census records of 1926, various economic surveys, and the uninformative published records of the Autonomous Volga German Republic comprise the bulk of the available sources. Materials pertinent to the collectivization and "dekulakization" of the German farmers, the purges of the late 1930s, and the forced removal of the Volga Germans during World War II presumably are still securely locked away in the innermost recesses of the labyrinthine Soviet repositories. Materials on Black Sea Germans during World War II can be found in German documents which later fell into Allied hands.[35]

Russian newspapers are valuable research aids, but they also have limitations and scholars should not expect too much. First, the government-controlled press forced editors to avoid certain topics, such as agrarian unrest. Government publications actually monopolized the press for the greater part of the nineteenth century. Privately owned newspapers at the provincial level did not appear in large numbers until the last quarter of the nineteenth century. So it is not until the turn of the century that the German settlers received much attention in the Russian press, with provincial newspapers showing most interest in the Germans. Naturally there appears to be a direct correlation between the number of German settlements and the extent of coverage they received in the local or provincial Russian press. Thus, the Saratov and Samara provincial press devoted more space to the densely settled Volga Germans than Tauride provincial newspapers allocated to the smaller and more scattered Black Sea colonies. Newspaper articles, however, add a human dimension to the statistically weighted government publications.

There are other primary sources on the German colonists too numerous to discuss in detail here. Very few personal memoirs are available relating to the German experience in Russia. Exceptionally interesting are the memoirs of Petr Karlovich Haller, written in 1918 (but not published until 1927), which describe daily life among the Volga Germans in the 1860s. A few tsarist officials, like Gavriil R. Derzhavin (the great classical poet) and Andrei M. Fadeev, briefly recollect their administrative experiences with the German colonists.[36]

Russian and Soviet Research

Russian and Soviet scholars have extensively, though not exhaustively, investigated the Germans in Russia. However, the quality of scholarship is varied, and the disparate enclaves of colonies in Bessarabia, Volynia, the Black Sea littoral, and the Volga region have not all shared the same historical scrutiny. Excellent original work has been done on the initial settlement and development of the colonies up to the mid-nineteenth century; on the other hand, very little is known about how the vital 1860–1880 period of reforms and the tsarist attempts to modernize Russia affected the Germans. The late 1880s witnessed the first manifestation of anticolonist tracts, which peaked during World War I. Soviet scholarship had barely begun to delve into the Germans' past when Stalin ordered the subject off limits to researchers. Finally, contemporary Soviet research is hampered by the continuing sensitivity of the subject and the concomitant danger of misinterpreting the present fluid Party policies toward the Soviet Germans.

Apollon Aleksandrovich Skal'kovskii pioneered Russian studies of the Germans in Russia with his prodigious collection and publication of information on New Russia. His two-volume *Khronologicheskoe obozrenie istorii novorossiiskago kraia, 1730–1823*, published in the 1830s, describes the 1804 founding of the German colonies in New Russia. Although his observations tend to be laudatory and general, he provides invaluable statistics (many collected personally) on the Bessarabian and Black Sea colonies. In his *Opyt statisticheskago opisaniia novorossiiskago kraia*, he provides a comprehensive account of the geography, history, ethnography, and settlement of New Russia. His paramount concern with agricultural developments in Russia's new frontier caused him to devote considerable attention to the advanced techniques and imported breeds of livestock of the foreign colonists.

In 1869 a russianized, Volga-born colonist, Aleksandr Avgustovich Klaus, published the first part of his pioneer study of foreign colonization in Russia, *Nashi kolonii* [Our Colonies].[37] Unfortunately, Klaus never realized his plans for a multi-volume general history, and Volume 1 remained the only volume ever published. The avowed didactic purpose of this book was to reveal to the Russian public the internal order and conditions of the colonies as a possible model for the Russian peasantry. Most Russians had heard of the colonies, "but only a score of people [were] closely familiar with the conditions of the internal organization and everyday life of this or that group of colonies. . . ."[38] Klaus proposed that "perhaps, the successes and failures of our colonists will help us to comprehend the real reasons for the disorder of our peasants, while indicating, at the same time, the means to improve their way of life."[39]

Nashi kolonii was based on erudite scholarship, but the author made no claim to comprehensiveness. Klaus had access to most of the relevant archives and direct administrative experience with the Volga colonies. However, he emphasized those colonies, such as the Mennonites, and those aspects of colonial life, primarily land tenure, that would best support his views. The Bessarabian colonies received little attention, and no serious attempt was made to unravel the social and economic arrangements of individual colonist households.

Klaus attempted to counter the arguments of an increasing number of critics attacking the colonies. He attributed criticism that the colonists had not served as a civilizing force for the neighboring native peasants to the two groups' deep social, political, and cultural divisions, not to the isolation of the colonies. The Black Sea colonists were individual, self-governing farmers, unlike their neighbors who, until 1861, had been serfs. Klaus also saw little correlation between the privileges originally granted the colonies and the colonies' prosperity. He retorted that most of the privileges had long expired and that similar groups had never achieved the same high level of economic success. He was dedicated to the idea that the colonial system of land tenure decreed in 1764, which combined individual use and hereditary possession with communal ownership, provided the key to the colonists' successes.[40] The productivity and efficiency of the consolidated, hereditary family holdings of the Black Sea colonies contrasted sharply with the system of periodically redistributed strips of land practiced in most peasant and Volga German communes. This former tsarist bureaucrat postulated that the colonial practice of individual land tenure and communal ownership could be decreed upon the recently emancipated serfs.

The 1880s witnessed the initial, but limited, outburst of anti–German literature in Russia. In 1889 and 1890, a series of articles written under the pseudonym of A. A. Velitsyn appeared in the journal *Russkii vestnik*; these articles were later republished in 1893 as a book entitled *Nemtsy v rossii*.[41] This undocumented, impressionistic account, based on a two-month visit to many of the German colonies, was a virulent polemic which vented the growing anti-German feeling in Russia by harshly attacking the German settlers as "fifth columnists." Velitsyn asserted that he would "outline the frightening strength of Germanism, advancing upon our Motherland like a dark cloud from the West, and which our German colonies serve as an obedient and active weapon."[42] The German economic stranglehold on Russia and the colonists' "seizure" of Russia's best lands forced Russians to wage a life-and-death struggle to rid Mother Russia of this alien element. Velitsyn's publications were so vitriolic that the German-language newspaper *St. Petersburger Zeitung* attempted to refute them.[43] In 1890 A. P. Liprandi also fanned anti-German feeling, and in 1891 a more restrained publication on German farmers' landholding in southern Russia nevertheless conveyed concern over the post-1860 expansion of German land acquisitions.[44] These publications were the first trickle of anti-German literature, which eventually inundated Russia during World War I.

Grigorii Pisarevskii wrote the best book on the subject of the immigration and early settlement of the Germans in Russia. He was the only Russian historian to devote the major part of his academic career to an investigation of foreign settlement in the tsarist empire.[45] In 1909, forty years after the publication of Klaus's volume, Pisarevskii published his dissertation, *Iz istorii inostrannoi kolonizatsii v rossii v XVIII v.* He recounted and interpreted the reasons for the Russian appeal to European peoples and their migration to Russia. Utilizing Russian archival materials, Pisarevskii attempted to place foreign settlement within the framework of the eighteenth-century enlightenment by discussing population theories and the colonization policies of Austria, Prussia, and Denmark. Although he exaggerated the influence of physiocratic ideas on Catherine II and her advisers, he lucidly supported the view that most eighteenth-century monarchs aggressively recruited foreign settlers.

Catherine II and her officials had conquered and opened up vast new territories, and Pisarevskii documented the fact that the Russian government spared nothing to attract colonists. The German colonies prospered and developed most successfully, but thousands of other nationals moved to Russia in the last quarter of the eighteenth century. When trouble arose in the Crimea, the government summoned Greeks and Armenians to settle there. Spain, having acquired the island of Minorca in 1781, exiled the Greeks and Corsicans who lived there. A Russian diplomat worked effectively to bring these people to the territory of New Russia. In the Danzig area dissatisfied Mennonites, unhappy with the city government's restrictions on their purchasing of land, were also recruited by a Russian agent to settle in Russia. Catherine's lover and trusted adviser, Gregory Potemkin, even thought about settling fugitive English convicts in the Crimea.

The outbreak of war with Germany in 1914 triggered a burst of German hate literature, which is historically interesting primarily for its insights into both the deep-seated fear of the Germans and the spy mania in Russia. German capitalists and the German settlers in Russia allegedly planned the economic subjugation of Russia to coincide with the conquest of Russia by Kaiser Wilhelm's advancing armies.[46] Journals, books, and newspaper articles carried the same message: the German settlers still retained their ancestral ties to Germany, yet continued to exploit the riches of Russia. The public outcry, the hate literature, and the government's desire to find scapegoats resulted in Duma land legislation inimical to the German settlers and in the confinement of German recruits in the tsarist army to rear services or the Turkish front.[47] Consequently, during the war little serious scholarship appeared on the Germans in Russia.

The 1920s marked a brief renaissance in German studies, but it was cut short by Stalin's imposition of ideological uniformity on all types of research. In 1922 Karl Lindemann, the University of Simferopol agronomist-zoologist, was instructed by the People's Commissariat of Nationalities to collect materials on the agrarian experiences of German colonists. Most of his findings were published abroad in *Von den deutschen Kolonisten in Russland; Ergebnisse einer Studienreise 1919–1921* (Stuttgart: Ausland und Heimat Verlags Aktiengesellschaft, 1924). The creation of the autonomous Volga German republic renewed interest in the Volga Germans. In 1926 E. Gross published an abbreviated study of the German-settled areas incorporated into the new republic.[48] The book chronicled the Volga Germans' struggle to survive the ravages of a bloody civil war, the famine of 1921–1922, and the flood of 1926. Gross's extensive reliance on statistics to quantify the region's postrevolutionary economic depression and the development of agricultural and industrial cooperatives makes this a very valuable source. Linguists are indebted to Viktor Maksimovich Zhirmunskii for his pioneering studies of the German dialects.[49] Finally, Valerian Obolenskii [Osinskii] devoted considerable attention in *Mezhdunarodnye i mezhkontinental'nye migratsii v dovoennoi rossii i SSSR* to the German emigration from Russia, which he attributed primarily to economic factors—land shortages, soil depletion, depressed agricultural prices, famine, and droughts, all compounded by German fecundity.

The stifling influence of Stalin on Russian historiography in general and his personal animosity towards the Germans in Russia lingers like a dark cloud. Khrushchev's destalinization and partial rehabilitation of the Soviet Germans have improved conditions for scholarly research, but serious research on the Germans is still insignificant and forced into the strait jacket of Marxist interpretation or buried in the works dealing with less sensitive topics. E. I. Druzhinina contributed two excellent monographs on the acquisition and settlement of the territory of New Russia in which she mentioned the German Black Sea colonies and the research accorded them by tsarist historians.[50] The *History of Moldavia* series [*Istoriia moldavii*] incorporated some documents relating to the German experience in Bessarabia.[51] Vladimir F. Shishmarev included a chapter on the Germans in Russia in his scholarly treatment of Romance language settlers in Russia.[52]

Soviet historians have been particularly reticent about the Volga Germans. Only V. V. Mavrodin has published an article specifically on the Volga Germans, and that was safely cloaked with a Marxist interpretation depicting most of the early Volga Germans as active revolutionaries in the Pugachev rebellion (1773–1774).[53] It is no accident that Soviet historians have not yet embarked on a study of the revolutionary and post-1917 periods in the German-populated Lower Volga region [*Nizhnee Povolzh'e*]. An abundant supply of studies exists on these periods on the Middle Volga region [*Srednee Povolzh'e*] (at least five books published between 1966 and 1974), but to my knowledge nothing comparable has been done on the Lower Volga region. Perhaps some time when the German issue is politically defused, Soviet authorities will sanction an extensive research effort on the Volga German and Black Sea German regions.

Form and Content of Entries

The arrangement of entries in this bibliography is by bibliographies, books and official publications, articles and statutes, and newspapers. All article and book titles have been translated into English, and annotations are given for those entries whose titles do not clearly reflect the scope or value of the publication. Entries have been prepared generally according to the style recommended by Kate L. Turabian, *A Manual for Writers of Term Papers, Theses and Dissertations* (4th ed., Chicago: University of Chicago Press, 1973) and *A Manual of Style* (12th ed. rev., Chicago: University of Chicago Press, 1969). A major exception is the citation of articles published in the *Zhurnal ministerstva gosudarstvennykh imushchestv* [Journal of the Ministry of State Domains]. The highly irregular pagination and numbering of volumes and sections in this journal necessitated the listing of articles exactly as they appear in the original. The Library of Congress system of transliteration and corporate entry has been generally used since most American libraries follow it. The only exceptions are some obscure items available only in the Soviet Union. In those cases the Lenin Library entry format has been given to assist researchers. Locational symbols used by the Library of Congress are given for each entry. Some entries, of course, are available in other libraries as well, but only the repositories known by the author to hold the entry are listed here. In the case of some multi-volume collections, volumes pertaining directly to major German settlements have been specifically listed under the main entry.

Every reasonable and practical effort was made to compile and present complete data for each entry and to render this bibliography as comprehensive, useful, and convenient as possible. Omissions exist— some known and, undoubtedly, others unknown. Soviet library catalogs are notoriously incomplete. The "public" catalog of the Lenin Library by no means approximates the complete library holdings. Nonetheless, in most cases of uncatalogued materials, Soviet librarians supplied the item if provided with the author and title of the work. The Soviet Union restricts research by western scholars to the major Soviet archives and libraries; undoubtedly, regional and local repositories contain vast, untapped materials. The sensitive nature of the topic impedes completeness; the reluctance of Soviet authorities to permit a close examination of the policies of the Stalin era has contributed to the dearth of entries listed with a post-1903 publication date. Sometimes obscure references provided the only source of incomplete information, and at other times dependence upon the bibliographic work of other compilers accounts for certain lapses of information. Finally, missing page numbers for some provincial newspapers are simply the result of the Lenin Library's transfer of its newspaper collection to another depository, which meant that many of the newspapers could not be circulated until cataloging was completed.

Notes

1. In 1764 the *Kantseliariia opekunstva inostrannykh poselentsev* was established in St. Petersburg to supervise foreign immigration and settlement in the Russian empire. In 1766 the Saratov office [*Kontora*] of the *Kantseliariia opekunstva inostrannykh poselentsev* assumed direct governmental supervision over the Volga colonies. Normally in the hands of Baltic Germans, who could communicate with the German-speaking settlers, the *Kontora* looked upon their clients as Russian landlords looked upon their serfs. In 1780 the *Kontora* was abolished and the foreign settlements became subject to local administration as a result of Catherine's provincial reforms. In 1797 the Saratov *Kontora* was reestablished because of provincial functionaries' ignorance of the foreigners' language and society. Although subordinate to the Ministry of State Domains beginning in 1837, the *Kontora* administered the Volga colonies until it was finally abolished in 1871.
2. Grigorii G. Pisarevskii, *Iz istorii inostrannoi kolonizatsii v rossii v XVIII v. (Po neizdannym arkhivnym dokumentam)* (Moscow: Pechatnia A. I. Snegirevyi, 1909), p. 177.
3. Vladimir F. Shishmarev, *Romanskie poseleniia na iuge rossii* (Leningrad: Izdatel'stvo "Nauka," 1975), p. 109.
4. In 1800 the tsarist government began preparing for foreign settlers in New Russia by establishing a *Kontora* in Ekaterinoslav, patterned after the Saratov *Kontora*. The Ekaterinoslav *Kontora* lasted until 1818, when it was replaced by the *Komitet opekunstva inostrannykh poselentsev*, which lasted until 1871. The *Komitet* assumed control of all foreign settlements in Kherson, Tauride, and Ekaterinoslav provinces, as well as Bessarabia.
5. Because of the inability of many of the original Volga settlers to repay government loans, the tsarist government became much stricter in screening prospective immigrants to New Russia. Consequently, the second wave of immigrants was more prosperous than the first.
6. Much of the anti-German feeling directed against the Black Sea settlements was generated by Ukrainian writers. See, for example, Sergei Shelukhin, *Nemetskaia kolonizatsiia na iuge rossii* (Odessa: Tip. aktsionernago iuzhno-russkago o-va pechatnago dela, 1915).
7. Russia, Ministerstvo gosudarstvennykh imushchestv, "Ob uspekhakh khoziaistva v koloniiakh iuzhnago kraia rossii," *Zhurnal ministerstva gosudarstvennykh imushchestv* chast' 23, otdel 2 (1847): 253.
8. A. A. Klaus, "Obshchina–sobstvennik i eia iuridicheskaia organizatsiia," *Vestnik evropy*, no. 2 (February 1870): 573–628; no. 3 (March 1870): 72–118.
9. *Zemstvos* were established in Samara Province in 1865 and in Saratov Province in 1866, the Volga region where most of the colonists lived. The *zemstvos* tried to control the German schools, rid them of the dominance of the German clergy, and introduce Russian as the language of instruction. See G. U., *Nemetskiia tserkovno-prikhodskiia uchilishcha v kamyshinskom uezde* (Saratov: Tipografiia gubernskago zemstva, n.d.), pp. 1–2.

19

10.   The law provided that every able-bodied male, irrespective of class, was liable for six years of military service when he reached the age of twenty. Actually, only about a third of those eligible were called. Since most of the Germans had some education, they would not have served six years, because educated males were granted reductions in length of service. University graduates served only six months; those with secondary education, two years; and graduates of primary schools, four years.

11.   G. U., *Nemetskiia tserkovno-prikhodskiia uchilishcha*, p. 3.

12.   David Rempel, "The Expropriation of the German Colonists in South Russia during the Great War," *Journal of Modern History* 4 (March 1932):49–67. A joke circulating in Russian newspapers about the alleged pervasiveness of German landholding in Russia went like this: Father: "Son, I, your papa, will give you two oranges, if you can tell me, where in our Holy Russia you cannot find Germans?" Son: "I don't know where." Father: "Where, indeed [don't the Germans live]!" See *Vechernee vremia*, 20 April/3 May 1915, p. 4.

13.   Aleksandr I. Solzhenitsyn, *The Gulag Archipelago*, trans. Thomas Whitney (New York: Harper & Row, 1974), vols. 1–2 (in one vol.), p. 138.

14.   "Nemtsev povolzh'ia avtonomnaia sovetskaia sotsialisticheskaia respublika (NPAAS)," *Bol'shaia sovetskaia entsiklopediia*, 1939 ed., vol. 41.

15.   Alexander Dallin, *German Rule in Russia 1941–1945: A Study of Occupation Policies* (London: Macmillan, 1957), p. 291.

16.   The outspoken Medvedev brothers asserted that the million Volga Germans deported to Kazakhstan in 1941 comprised the basic permanent work force which carried out Khrushchev's "virgin lands" program in the 1950s, and therefore, it was economically inexpedient to allow them to return to their homes along the Volga. See Roy A. and Zhores A. Medvedev, *Khrushchev: The Years in Power*, trans. Andrew R. Durkin (New York: Columbia University Press, 1976), p. 122. Fred C. Koch substantiated this view in *The Volga Germans in Russia and the Americas, from 1763 to the Present* (University Park and London: Pennsylvania State University Press, 1977), p. 301. Koch also reported (p. 294) that despite the government ban prohibiting a return to the Volga region, a few Volga Germans have returned to former colony sites.

17.   There are two other regionally published German newspapers. *Freundschaft* is a daily newspaper specially for Germans living in Kazakhstan. *Rote Fahne* is published for Germans living in the Altai Territory.

18.   On 8 March 1977, ten former Volga German residents were arrested for demonstrating in Red Square and demanding the right to emigrate.

19.   B. A. Rybakov, *Istoriia SSSR s drevneishikh vremen do kontsa XVIII veka* (Moscow: Izdatel'stvo "Vysshaia shkola," 1975), p. 366.

20.   Ibid., pp. 468–70.

21.   Among Soviets with whom I spoke, there was a genuine ignorance of the German colonists and their forced deportation during World War II.

22.   *Papa Dell and His Family—The Life of Soviet Citizens of German Origin* (Moscow: Novosti Press Agency Publishing House, 1975), p. 8.

23.   Patricia Grimsted, *Archives and Manuscript Repositories in the USSR: Moscow and Leningrad* (Princeton: Princeton University Press, 1972), pp. 168–82. The arrangement and composition of the records of the Ministry of State Domains is found in P. A. Shafranov, comp., *Arkhiv ministerstva zemledeliia i gosudarstvennykh imushchestv (istoricheskii ocherk ustroistva i sostav del)* (St. Petersburg: Tipografiia V. F. Kirshbauma, 1904).

24.   A. A. Geraklitov, "Arkhivy saratovskoi gubernii," *Trudy saratovskoi uchenoi arkhivnoi komissii*, no. 30 (1913): 16.

25.   Other important individual legislative acts pertaining to the German-Russians are listed in the article and statute section of this bibliography under Russia. Laws, statutes, etc. *Polnoe sobranie zakonov rossiiskoi imperii*.

26.   See especially, Russia, Ministerstvo gosudarstvennykh imushchestv, "Istoriia i statistika kolonii inostrannykh poselentsev v rossii," *Zhurnal ministerstva gosudarstvennykh im-*

ushchestv, chast' 52, otdel 2 (1854): 36–78; chast' 53, otdel 2 (1854): 1–34; chast' 54, otdel 1(1855): chast' 55, otdel 1(1855):57–88, 121–37. This journal has very irregular pagination.

27.   In the appendix to his work, *Nashi kolonii* (pp. 45–59), A.A. Klaus printed some statistics taken from the last six revisions on the colonists in Saratov and Samara Provinces. Fifth revision materials are found in the Central State Archive on Ancient Acts [*Tsentral'nyi gosudarstvennyi arkhiv drevnikh aktov*] and the Central State Historical Archive [*Tsentral'nyi gosudarstvennyi istoricheskii arkhiv*](TsGIA), fonds 248 and 571 respectively. Revisions 6 through 10 are located in fond 571 of the Central State Historical Archive.

28.   Russia, Tsentral'nyi statisticheskii komitet, *Spiski naselennykh mest rossiiskoi imperii, sostavlennye i izdavaemye tsentral'nym statisticheskim komitetom ministerstva vnutrennikh del. (Po svedeniiam 1859)*, 47 vols. in 42. (St. Petersburg: Tipografiia Karl Vul'f,1861–85.). In addition to the above, three other serial publications of the Central Statistical Committee are quite valuable. They are *Statisticheskii vremennik rossiiskoi imperii* (issued from 1866 to 1890), *Statistika pozemel'noi sobstvennosti i naselennykh mest* (issued from 1880 to 1885), and *Statistika rossiiskoi imperii* (issued from 1887 to 1914).

29.   The next general census was not conducted until 1926 by the Soviet government. See Russia (1923–USSR), Tsentral'noe statisticheskoe upravlenie, Otdel perepisi, *Vsesoiuznaia perepis' naseleniia 1926 goda*, 57 vols. (Moscow: TsSu, 1928–33).

30.   Vasilii N. Grigor'ev, *Predmetnyi ukazatel' materialov v zemsko-statisticheskikh trudakh s 1860-kh godov po 1917 g.*, 2 vols. (Moscow: Tsentral'noe statisticheskoe upravlenie SSSR, 1926–27); V. F. Karavaev, *Bibliograficheskii obzor zemskoi statisticheskoi i otsenochnoi literatury so vremeni uchrezhdeniia zemstv' 1864–1903 g.*, 2 vols. (St. Petersburg: vol. 1, Tipo-litografiia M. P. Frolova, 1906; vol. 2, Tipo-litografiia N. L. Nyrkina, 1913).

31.   See, for example, *Sbornik statisticheskikh svedenii po tavricheskoi gubernii*, 9 vols. (Simferopol: Tavricheskoe gubernskoe zemstvo, 1885–89).

32.   B. D. Al'man, "Vliianie trakhomy na ekonomicheskoe polozhenie poselian' nemetskikh kolonii," *Vestnik novouzenskago zemstva*, no. 3 (May-June 1912): 70–80; and G. I. Kolesnikov, "Novouzenskii uezd (v ego proshlom i nastoiashchem)," *Vestnik novouzenskago zemstva*, no. 2 (March-April 1912): 35.

33.   Valerian V. Obolenskii [Osinskii], *Mezhdunarodnye i mezhkontinental'nye migratsii v dovoennoi rossii i SSSR* (Moscow: Tsentral'noe statisticheskoe upravlenie SSSR, 1928), p. 7. Even the United States immigration authorities did not record both the country and the nationality of the immigrant until 1899.

34.   U.S., Congress, Senate, *Senate Documents*, Reports of the Immigration Commission, *Emigration Conditions in Europe*, 12, 61st Cong., 3rd sess., 1911, pp. 239–348.

35.   Dallin cites many of them in his *German Rule in Russia, 1941–1945.*

36.   Petr Karlovich Haller, *Vospominaniia P. K. Gallera. (Byt nemtsev-kolonistov v 60-kh godakh XIX veka)* (Saratov, 1927). Gavriil Romanovich Derzhavin, *Sochineniia Derzhavina* (St. Petersburg: Imperatorskaia akademiia nauk, 1869), vol. 5, ed. Iakov Karlovich Grot. Andrei M. Fadeev, "Vospominaniia Andreia Mikhailovicha Fadeeva," *Russkii arkhiv*, no. 4 (1891): 465-94; no. 5 (1891): 14–60.

37.   Aleksandr Avgustovich Klaus was unique. Born the son of an organist in one of the Volga German colonies in Saratov Province, he graduated from the Saratov *gymnasium* and entered government service in the Saratov office of the Guardianship of Foreign Settlers. In 1863 he moved to St. Petersburg and continued service in the Ministry of State Domains. In 1871, after thirteen years' service in the ministry, Klaus transferred to the Ministry of Communications, and in 1874 he became Vice Director of the Department of Highways and Waterways. He retired from state service in 1876 and died in the late 1870s. Interestingly, his brother Avgust Avgustovich Klaus also pursued a government career in the Volga area as a court investigator in the district and provincial court system.

38.   A. A. Klaus, *Nashi kolonii. Opyty materialy po istorii i statistike inostrannoi kolonizatsii v rossii* (St. Petersburg: Tipografiia V. V. Nusval't, 1869), p. 1.

39.   Ibid., p. 3.

40.   Klaus pursued the same theme in "Obshchina-sobstvennik i eia iuridicheskaia organizatsiia," *Vestnik evropy*, no. 2 (February 1870): 573–628; no. 3 (March 1870): 72–118.

41.   A. A. Velitsyn, pseud. [A. A. Paltov], *Nemtsy v rossii; ocherki istoricheskago razvitiia i nastoiashchago polozheniia nemetskikh kolonii na iuge i vostoke rossii* (St. Petersburg: Izdanie russkago vestnika, 1893).

42.   A. A. Velitsyn, pseud. [A. A. Paltov], *Nemetskoe zavoevanie na iuge rossii* (St. Petersburg: Tipografiia tovarishchestva "Obshchestvennaia Pol'za," 1890), p. 3.

43.   See *St. Petersburger Zeitung*, 1889, no. 39, 162, 165; 1890, no. 17, 20, 44, 46.

44.   A. P. Liprandi, pseud. [A. Volynets], *Kak ostanovit' mirnoe zavoevanie nashikh okrain? Nemetskii vopros, sushchnost' i znachenie ego v iugo-zapadnoi rossii* (Kiev: Tipografiia gen. Bruna, 1890); Lev Vasil'evich Padalka, *Zemlevladenie nemtsev, byvshikh kolonistov v khersonskoi gubernii* (Kherson: Izdanie khersonskoe gubernskoe zemstvo, 1891).

45.   Pisarevskii studied at Moscow State University, where his doctoral dissertation received the Karpov prize. He later taught at the University of Warsaw and Azerbaidzhan State University. He continued his academic career under the Bolsheviks, but his final fate is unknown to this author. In addition to his monograph on foreign settlement in Russia, Pisarevskii also wrote numerous articles on the subject.

46.   Examples of this anti-German literature are A. A. Dunin, "V nemetskikh kogtiakh. Povest'. (Iz staro-moskovskago nemetskago zasil'ia)," *Istoricheskii vestnik* 149–50 (January 1917): 1–35; M. V. Murav'ev, ed., *"Nemetskoe zlo" sbornik statei posviashchennykh voprosu o bor'be s nashei "vnutrennei germaniei"* (Moscow: Tipografiia A. I. Mamontov, 1915); A. M. Rennikov, *Zoloto reina o nemtsakh v rossii* (Petrograd: Tipografiia T-va A. S. Suvorin, 1915); Ivan Ivanovich Sergeev, *Mirnoe zavoevanie rossii nemtsami (doklad, prochitannyi v chrezvychainom obshchem sobranii g. g. chlenov "Obshchestva 1914 goda" 13 marta 1915 goda)* (Petrograd: Tipo-litografiia N. I. Evstifeev, 1915); and Grigorii A. Yevreinov, *Rossiiskie nemtsy* (Petrograd: Tip. Glavnago upravleniia udelov, 1915).

47.   The legislation limiting German landholding in Russia is examined in Karl Eduardovich Lindeman, *Prekrashchenie zemlevladeniia i zemlepol'zovaniia poselian' sobstvennikov. Ukazy 2 fevralia i 13 dekabria 1915 goda i 10, 15 iiulia i 19 avgusta 1916 goda i ikh vliianie na ekonomicheskoe sostoianie iuzhnoi rossii* (Moscow: K. L. Men'shova, 1917).

48.   E. Gross, *Avt. sots. sov. resp. nemtsev povolzh'ia* (Pokrovsk: Nemgosizdat, 1926). See also V. Kleiman, "Avtonomnaia oblast' nemtsev povolzh'ia," *Zhizn' natsional'nostei* 1 (January 1923): 62–67; Grigorii I. Nabatov, *Respublika bez mezhei: respublika nemtsev povolzh'ia* (Moscow: Priboi, 1930) and Al. Rakitnikov, "U nemetskikh kolonistov," *Krasnaia nov'*, no. 9 (November 1925): 243–49.

49.   V. M. Zhirmunskii led the way in dialect studies. See his "Problemy kolonial'noi dialektologii," *Iazyk i literatura*, no. 3 (1929): 179–220; "Itogi i zadachi dialektologicheskogo i etnograficheskogo izucheniia nemetskikh poselenii SSSR," *Sovetskaia etnografiia*, no. 2 (1933): 84–112; and "Vostochno-srednenemetskie govory i problema smesheniia dialektov," *Iazyk i myshlenie* 6–7 (1936): 133–59.

50.   E. I. Druzhinina, *Iuzhnaia ukraina v 1800–1825 gg.* (Moscow: Izdatel'stvo "Nauka," 1970) and *Severnoe prichernomor'e v 1775–1800 gg.* (Moscow: Izdatel'stvo akademii nauk SSSR, 1959).

51.   Akademiia nauk moldavskoi SSR, Institut istorii, *Istoriia moldavii*. Vol. 3, no. 2: *Polozhenie krest'ian i krest'ianskoe dvizhenie v bessarabii (1812–1861 gody). Sbornik dokumentov* (Kishinev: Izdatel'stvo TsKKP Moldavii, 1969).

52.   Vladimir F. Shishmarev, *Romanskie poseleniia na iuge rossii* (Leningrad: Izdatel'stvo "Nauka," 1975).

53.   V. V. Mavrodin, "Ob uchastii kolonistov povolzh'ia v vosstanii Pugacheva," in *Krest'ianstvo i klassovaia bor'ba v feodal'noi rossii*, ed. by N. E. Nosov (Leningrad: Izdatel'stvo "Nauka," 1967), pp. 400–413.

List of Libraries and Symbols

CSt-H Hoover Institution on War, Peace and Revolution (Stanford)

CtY   Yale University (New Haven)

CU   University of California (Berkeley)

DLC   Library of Congress (Washington, D.C.)

LL   Lenin Library (Moscow)

NcD   Duke University (Durham)

NN   New York Public Library (New York City)

NNC   Columbia University (New York City)

Bibliographies

I. Bibliographies

1. Grigor'ev, Vasilii Nikolaevich. *Predmetnyi ukazatel' materialov v zemsko-statisticheskikh trudakh s 1860-kh godov po 1917 g.* 2 vols. Moscow: Tsentral'noe statisticheskoe upravlenie SSSR, 1926, 1927.

DLC NN

Subject Index of Materials in Zemstvo Statistical Works from 1860 to 1917.

Zemstvo materials contain invaluable information about the German settlers in Russia. This is an indispensable guide to *zemstvo* publications.

2. Iakushkin, Evgenii Ivanovich. *Obychnoe pravo; materialy dlia bibliografii obychnago prava.* 4 vols. Yaroslavl: various publishers, 1875, 1896, 1908, 1910.

DLC

Customary Law: Materials for a Bibliography of Customary Law.

Most extensive annotated index of books and articles on customary law in Russia with several references to the Germans in Russia. Volumes 1 and 3 now available in microfiche.

3. Karavaev, V. F. *Bibliograficheskii obzor zemskoi statisticheskoi i otsenochnoi literatury so vremeni uchrezhdeniia zemstv' 1864–1903 g.* St. Petersburg: Tipo–litografiia M. P. Frolova and N. L. Nyrkina, 1906, 1913.

DLC

A Bibliographical Review of Zemstvo Statistical and Evaluative Literature from the Time of the Establishment of Zemstvos, 1864–1903.

An invaluable reference to *zemstvo* publications.

4. Köppen, Petr Ivanovich, comp. *Khronologicheskii ukazatel' materialov dlia istorii inorodtsev evropeiskoi rossii*. St. Petersburg: Tipografiia imperatorskoi akademii nauk, 1861.

DLC

A Chronological Index of Materials for the History of Foreigners in European Russia.

A chronological ordering of information from *Russkiia letopisi*, Karamzin's *Istoriia gosudarstva rossiiskago*, *Sobranie gosudarstvennykh gramot i dogovorov*, *Akty arkheograficheskoi ekspeditsii (1836 goda)*, *Akty archkeograficheskoi kommissii*, *Akty iuridicheskie*, *Polnoe sobranie zakonov*, and a few other publications. Covers twenty-nine non-Russian peoples including the German settlers.

5. Mezhov, Vladimir I. *Bibliograficheskii ukazatel' vyshedshikh v 1859 godu, v rossii, knig i statei po chasti geografii, topografii, etnografii i statistiki*. St. Petersburg: Tipografiia V. Bezobrazova, 1861.

NN

Bibliographic Index of Books and Articles Published in 1859 on the Subjects of Geography, Topography, Ethnography, and Statistics.

This bibliography includes numerous obscure references to the Germans in Russia.

6. Mezhov, Vladimir I. *Literatura russkoi geografii, statistiki i etnografii za 1877 god*. St. Petersburg: Tipografiia V. Bezobrazova, 1880, vol. 8, pt. 1.

NN

Russian Geographical, Statistical, and Ethnographical Literature for the Year 1877.

An extensive bibliography of contemporary historical literature, which contains many periodical literature citations on the German settlements.

7. Mezhov, Vladimir I. *Literatura russkoi geografii, statistiki i etnografii za 1878 god*. St. Petersburg: Tipografiia V. Bezobrazova, 1881, vol. 8, pt. 2.

NN

Russian Geographical, Statistical, and Ethnographical Literature for the Year 1878.

See annotation for entry 6.

8. Mezhov, Vladimir I. *Literatura russkoi geografii, statistiki i etnografii za 1879 god.* St. Petersburg: Tipografiia V. Bezobrazova, 1882, vol. 9, pt 1.
NN
Russian Geographical, Statistical, and Ethnographical Literature for the Year 1879.

See annotation for entry 6.

9. Mezhov, Vladimir I. *Russkaia istoricheskaia bibliografiia. Ukazatel' knig i statei po russkoi i vseobshchei istorii i vspomogatel'nym naukam za 1800–1854 vkl.* Vol. 3. St. Petersburg: Tipografiia I. N. Skorokhodova, 1893.
NN
A Russian Historical Bibliography: Index of Books and Articles on Russian and World History and Auxiliary Sciences for the Years 1800–1854.

A monumental bibliography which includes numerous references to the foreign settlements in Russia. An invaluable research tool.

10. Russia. Ministerstvo gosudarstvennykh imushchestv. *Alfavitnyi ukazatel' statei zhurnala ministerstva gosudarstvennykh imushchestv za odinnadtsat let s 1857 po 1868 god.* St. Petersburg: Tipografiia imperatorskoi akademii nauk, 1869.
LL
An Alphabetical Index of Articles in the Journal of State Domains for the Eleven Years from 1857 through 1868.

See annotation for entry 11.

11. Russia. Ministerstvo gosudarstvennykh imushchestv. *Alfavitnyi ukazatel' statei zhurnala ministerstva gosudarstvennykh imushchestv za shestnadtsat let s 1841 po 1856 god vkliuchitel'no.* Compiled by A. Zablotskii. St. Petersburg: Tipografiia imperatorskoi akademii nauk, 1858.
LL
An Alphabetical Index of Articles in the Journal of the Ministry of State Domains for the Sixteen Years from 1841 through 1856.

A very useful but rarely found index of the official journal of the Ministry of State Domains, which was the agency in charge of the foreign colonies in Russia for much of the nineteenth century.

12. Schiller, Frants P. *Literatura po istorii nemetskikh kolonii v SSSR za vremia 1764–1926 g.g./ Literatur zu Geschichte und Volkskunde der deutschen Kolonien in der Sowet-Union für die Jahre 1764–1926*. Pokrovsk: Tipografiia Nemgosizdat, 1927.

NN

Literature on the History of the German Colonies in the USSR for the Period 1764-1926.

Excellent bibliography which contains 957 German and Russian language entries with most in German.

13. Val'denberg, D. V., comp. *Spravochnaia kniga o pechati vsei rossii*. St. Petersburg: "T-vo khudozhestvennoi pechati," 1911.

LL

Reference Book for the Press of Russia.

Very good reference tool for information on the provincial and district-level newspapers and journals in Russia.

Books and Official Publications

II. Books and Official Publications

14. Akademiia nauk moldavskoi SSR. Institut istorii. *Istoriia moldavii* vol. 3, no. 2: *Polozhenie krest'ian i krest'ianskoe dvizhenie v bessarabii (1812–1861 gody). Sbornik dokumentov.* Kishinev: Izdatel'stvo TsKKP Moldavii, 1969.

DLC NN

History of Moldavia. The Condition of the Peasantry and the Peasant Movement in Bessarabia (1812–1861): A Collection of Documents.

Includes some documents on the foreign colonies in Bessarabia.

15. Akademiia nauk SSSR. Institut geografii. *Povolzh'e; ekonomiko-geograficheskaia kharakteristika.* Edited by K. V. Dolgopolov and V. V. Pokshishevskii. Moscow: Gos. izdatel'stvo geograficheskoi literatury, 1957.

DLC NN

The Volga Region: Economic-Geographic Characteristics.

16. Akkermanskoe zemstvo. *Statisticheskoe opisanie bessarabii sobstvenno tak nazyvaemoi ili budzhaka s prilozheniem general'nago plana ego kraia.* Akkerman: Tipografiia I. M. Grinshteina, 1899.

LL

Statistical Description of Bessarabia Properly Called or Budzhak with an Appendix of the General Plan of the Region.

Contains population figures on the foreign colonies in Bessarabia. Coverage of the book is up to 1828 with emphasis on the period of the Russian empire (1812–1828). It had been tucked away in archives until found and published by the Akkerman *zemstvo* in 1899.

17. Bagalei, Dmitrii Ivanovich. *Kolonizatsiia novorossiiskago kraia i pervye shagi ego po puti kul'tury. Istoricheskii etiud.* Kiev: Tipografiia G. T. Korchak-Novitskago, 1889.

DLC

The Colonization of the Region of New Russia and Its First Steps on the Way to Culture: A Historical Study.

Covers the settlement of New Russia by the Cossacks and foreign colonists, including Serbs, Greeks, Germans, and Armenians. Section on foreign settlement is quite short, but the work provides useful information on the overall settlement of New Russia.

18. Bagalei, Dmitrii Ivanovich. *Ocherki iz istorii kolonizatsii i byta stepnoi okrainy moskovskago gosudarstva.* Moscow: Izdanie imperatorskago obshchestva istorii i drevnostei rossiiskikh pri moskovskom universitete, 1887.

CU

Essays on the History of the Colonization and Life of the Steppe Borderland of the Muscovite State.

This work deals with the Russian colonization of the borderland regions around Voronezh, Kursk, and Kharkov from the beginning of the Muscovite state through the reign of Alexis Romanov.

19. Batiushkov, Pompeii Nikolaevich. *Bessarabiia istoricheskoe opisanie.* St. Petersburg: Tipografiia "Obshchestvennaia Pol'za," 1892.

DLC NN

Bessarabia: A Historical Description.

A brief history of Bessarabia which mentions the role of foreign colonization in the settlement and development of the region.

20. Bogoslovskii, Mikhail M. *Istoriia rossii XVIII veka, 1725–1796.* Moscow: Obshchestvo vzaimopomoshchi studentov-filologov pri imperatorskom universitete, 1915.

CSt-H

A History of Russia in the Eighteenth Century, 1725–1796.

A general history of the period by a leading authority on Peter the Great. Briefly discusses Potemkin's plans to settle New Russia with European colonists.

21.   Bondar, S. D. *Sekta mennonitov v rossii v sviazi s istoriei nemetskoi kolonizatsii na iuge rossii.* Petrograd: Tipografiia V.D. Smirnova, 1916.
CSt-H DLC NN
The Mennonite Sect in Russia in Connection with the History of the German Colonization in Southern Russia.

Excellent book on Mennonite settlement in Russia which also devotes considerable attention to German immigration to Russia.

22.   Bruckner, Alexander. *Potemkin.* St. Petersburg: K. L. Rikkeia, 1891.
CSt-H
Potemkin.

Biography of the man mainly responsible for the settlement of New Russia during the reign of Catherine II.

23.   Chelintsev, Aleksandr N., ed. *Sbornik statisticheskikh materialov po voprosam organizatsii krest'ianskogo khoziaistva ukrainy i smezhnykh gubernii.* Odessa: Narodnyi komissariat zemledeliia ukrainy, 1922.
CSt-H
A Collection of Statistical Materials relating to the Question of the Organization of the Peasant Economy of the Ukraine and Adjoining Provinces.

This collection contains provincial, district, and volost agricultural statistics on the provinces of Chernigov, Kursk, Voronezh, Kharkov, Poltava, Kherson, Ekaterinoslav, Tauride, and the Don Forces Oblast.

24.   Den', Vladimir Eduardovich, ed. *Khoziaistvennaia statistika SSSR; sbornik statei.* Leningrad: Priboi, 1930.
CSt-H
Economic Statistics of the Soviet Union: A Collection of Articles.

25.   Den', Vladimir Eduardovich. *Naselenie rossii po piatoi revizii.* 2 vols. Moscow: Universitetskaia tipografiia, 1902.
LL
The Population of Russia Based on the Fifth Revision.

Evaluates the first five revisions as source materials.

26.   Derzhavin, Gavriil Romanovich. *Sochineniia Derzhavina*. St. Petersburg: Tipografiia imperatorskaia akademiia nauk, 1869, vol. 5, edited by Iakov Karlovich Grot.

                                                             DLC NN

The Works of Derzhavin.

This volume relates the experiences of the great classical poet during the Pugachev rebellion, when he was a government official stationed not too far from the Volga German colonies.

27.   Drabkina, Elizaveta Ia. *Natsional'nyi i kolonial'nyi vopros v tsarskoi rossii*. Moscow: Izdatel'stvo kommunisticheskoi akademii, 1930.

                                                             CSt-H DLC

The National and Colonial Question in Tsarist Russia.

Includes several articles on the nationality question and has one of the best bibliographies on the subject.

28.   Druzhinin, Nikolai M. *Gosudarstvennye krest'iane i reformá P. D. Kiseleva*. 2 vols. Moscow-Leningrad: Izdatel'stvo akademii nauk SSSR, 1946, 1958.

                                                             DLC NN

The State Peasants and the Reform of P. D. Kiselev.

The definitive work on the subject. Provides excellent background on conditions in rural Russia from 1800 to 1840.

29.   Druzhinina, E. I. *Iuzhnaia ukraina v 1800–1825 gg*. Moscow: Izdatel'stvo "Nauka," 1970.

                                                             DLC NN

The Southern Ukraine from 1800 to 1825.

Outstanding work by a Soviet scholar, which has a very extensive bibliographic essay that includes sources on the German settlers.

30.   Druzhinina, E. I. *Severnoe prichernomor'e v 1775–1800 gg*. Moscow: Izdatel'stvo akademii nauk SSSR, 1959.

                                                             DLC NN

The Northern Black Sea Area, 1775–1800.

The authoritative work on the northern Black Sea provinces for this period. Based on numerous Soviet archives with extensive references to provincial archives.

31. Dubrovin, N. F. *Pugachev i ego soobshchniki (Epizod iz istorii tsarstvovaniia Imperatritsy Ekateriny II) 1773–1774 gg.* Vol. 3. St. Petersburg: Tipografiia I. N. Skorokhodova, 1884.

DLC NN

Pugachev and His Confederates (An Episode from the History of the Reign of Empress Catherine II), 1773–1774.

Chapter 12 deals with Pugachev and the Volga German colonists.

32. Ekaterinburgskoe gubernskoe statisticheskoe biuro. *Spisok naselennykh punktov ekaterinburgskoi gubernii s vazhneishimi statisticheskimi dannymi i alfavitnym ukazatelem.* Ekaterinburg: Mart., 1923.

LL

A List of Populated Points of Ekaterinburg Province with the Most Important Statistical Data and an Alphabetical Index.

33. Engel'gardt, A. P. *Ocherk krest'ianskogo khoziaistva v kazanskoi i drugikh sredne-volzhskikh guberniiakh.* Kazan: Tipo–litografiia imperatorskago universiteta, 1892.

DLC

An Essay on Peasant Households in Kazan and Other Middle Volga Provinces.

Detailed study of the problems of peasant agriculture in the Middle Volga (primarily Kazan Province) with suggestions for improvement.

34. Firsov, Nikolai. *Inorodcheskoe naselenie prezhniago kazanskago tsarstva v novoi rossii do 1762 goda i kolonizatsiia zakamskiikh zemel' v eto vremia.* Kazan: Universitetskaia tipografiia, 1869.

DLC

The Foreign Population of the Former Kingdom of Kazan in New Russia up to 1762 and the Colonization of the Trans-Kama Territory at This Time.

History of the peoples living in the region before the arrival of the Volga Germans.

35. G. U. *Nemetskiia tserkovno-prikhodskiia uchilishcha v kamyshinskom uezde.* Saratov: Tipografiia gubernskago zemstva, n.d.

LL

German Church-Parish Schools in Kamyshin District.

This account of church-parish schools in Kamyshin District, Saratov Province, states that it is a reprint from the *Saratovskaia zemskaia nedelia za 1900,* no. 1–10.

36. Georgi, Johann Gottlieb. *Opisanie vsekh obitaiushchikh v rossiiskom gosudarstve narodov.* 4 vols. St. Petersburg: Izhdiveniem I. Glazunova pri imperatorskoi akademii nauk, 1799.

DLC NN

Description of All Peoples Inhabiting the Russian Empire.

Ethnographic study of peoples of European Russia, Siberia, and some borderlands. Originally published in German as *Beschreibung aller Nationen des russischen Reichs,* 2 vols. (St. Petersburg, 1776–1780). The Russian text amends the original German text.

37. Geraklitov, A. A. *Istoriia saratovskogo kraia v XVI–XVIII vekakh.* Saratov: Izdatel'stvo saratovskogo obshchestva istorii, arkheologii i etnografii, 1923.

LL

History of the Saratov Region from the Sixteenth to Eighteenth Centuries.

Very useful history of the Volga region before the arrival of the foreign settlers.

38. German Volga ASSR. Gosudarstvennaia planovaia komissiia. *Itogi narodno-khoziaistvennogo stroitel'stva ASSR NP za 15 let (1918–1933 g.).* Engel's: Nemgosizdat, 1933.

LL

Results of National Economic Construction of the Autonomous Soviet Socialist Republic of the Volga Germans for Fifteen Years (1918–1933).

A general Soviet survey of the economic development of the German Volga ASSR.

39. German Volga ASSR. Konstitutsiia. 1937. *Konstitutsiia (osnovnoi zakon) avtonomnoi sovetskoi sotsialisticheskoi respubliki nemtsev povolzh'ia.* Engel's: Gosizdat ASSRNP, 1937.

DLC

The Constitution (Fundamental Law) of the Autonomous Soviet Socialist Republic of Volga Germans.

40. German Volga ASSR. Laws, statutes, etc. *O gosudarstvennom plane vesennego seva 1937 goda. Ob organizatsii posevov prosa chistosortnymi semenami i ob uluchshenii semenovodstva po prosu.* Engel's, 193–.

DLC

The State Sowing Plan of 1937: Organization of Millet Sowing, Seed Selection and Improvement of Millet Seed Sowing.

Technical report on millet planting in the Volga German region.

41. German Volga ASSR. Narodnyi komissariat prosveshcheniia. *Sel'skokhoziaistvennyi uklon v prosvetitel'nykh uchrezhdeniiakh; tezisy i doklad narkoma prosveshcheniia tov. Shenfel'd.* Pokrovsk: Izd. narodnogo komissariata zemledeliia ASSRNP, 1929.

DLC

Agricultural Education in Educational Institutions: Theses and Report of the People's Committee of Education by Comrade Shenfel'd.

Contains materials for the conference in Pokrovsk (15–21 January 1929) to upgrade agricultural education.

42. German Volga ASSR. Narodnyi komissariat zemledeliia. *Agropravila dlia kolkhozov ASSR Nemtsev Povolzh'ia. Proekt Narkomzema ASSR Nemtsev Povolzh'ia.* Engel's: Narkomzem ASSRNP, 1938.

LL

Agriculture Regulations for the Collective Farms of the Autonomous Soviet Socialist Republic of the Volga Germans. Draft of the People's Commissariat of Agriculture of the Autonomous Soviet Socialist Republic of the Volga Germans.

43. German Volga ASSR. Oblast' nemtsev povolzh'ia. *Otchet ekonomicheskogo soveshchaniia oblasti nemtsev povolzh'ia. Na 1-e aprelia 1922 g.* Pokrovsk: Tipografiia obsovnarkhoza, 1922.

NNC

Report of the Economic Conference of the Region of Volga Germans, 1
April 1922.

Intended to be a short narrative (but primarily a statistical presentation)
of economic conditions in the German Volga region of the RSFSR
(Russian Soviet Federated Socialist Republic) in April 1922.

44.   German Volga ASSR. S'ezd sovetov, 4–i. *Postanovleniia IV-go s'ezda
sovetov avtonomnoi sovetskoi sotsialisticheskoi respubliki nemtsev povolzh'ia.*
Pokrovsk: TsIK ASSRNP, 1927.
                                                                       LL
Resolutions of the Fourth Session of the Soviet of the Autonomous
Soviet Socialist Republic of the Volga Germans.

45.   German Volga ASSR. S'ezd sovetov, 7–i. *Postanovleniia VII s'ezda
sovetov rabochikh, krest'ianskikh batratskikh i krasnoarmeiskikh deputatov
ASSRNP i 1-i sessii tsentral'nogo ispolnitel'nogo komiteta sozyva Avt.
SSRNP.* Pokrovsk: druck. des ZVWR der ASSR der WD, 1929.
                                                                       LL
Resolutions of the Seventh Congress of Soviets of Workers, Peasants,
Farm Laborers, and Red Army Deputies of the ASSRNP and the First
Session of the Central Executive Committee of the Seventh Convoca-
tion of the Autonomous SSRNP.

46.   German Volga ASSR. Statisticheskoe upravlenie. *Biullentin' statisticheskogo upravleniia.* Pokrovsk: Izdatel'stvo statisticheskogo upravleniia
resp. nemtsev povolzh'ia, 1925.
                                                                    CSt-H
Bulletin of the Statistical Administration of the German Volga ASSR.

This statistical bulletin appeared irregularly during the 1920s. Its primary focus was on the economic development of the republic.

47.   German Volga ASSR. Statisticheskoe upravlenie. *Predvaritel'nye itogi
vsesoiuznoi perepisi naseleniia 1926 goda po avton. sots. sov. respublike nemtsev
povolzh'ia.* Pokrovsk: Tipografiia nemgosizdata, 1927.
                                                                     DLC
Preliminary Results of the 1926 All-Union Population Census of the
Autonomous Soviet Socialist Republic of Volga Germans.

1926 population census figures for the German autonomous republic
with the text in Russian and German.

48. German Volga ASSR. Statisticheskoe upravlenie. *Sbornik statisticheskikh svedenii po avtonomnoi sotsialisticheskoi sovetskoi respublike nemtsev povolzh'ia, 1916–1924 gg.* Pokrovsk: Tsentral'noe statisticheskoe upravlenie ASSRNP, 1924.

LL

A Collection of Statistical Information on the Autonomous Soviet Socialist Republic of the Volga Germans, 1916–1924.

Although the statistical data is not broken down by administrative sub-units of the German Volga ASSR, the general figures cover such subjects as population, industry, crop acreage, homesteads, and literacy.

49. German Volga ASSR. Tsentral'noe biuro nauchnogo izucheniia dialektov ASSRNP. *K kharakteristike ukrainskikh govorov respubliki nemtsev povolzh'ia.* Edited by A. Dul'son and G. Dinges. Pokrovsk: Deutscher Staatsverlag der ASS Respublik der Wolgadeutschen, 1927.

NN

Characteristics of Ukrainian Dialects in the Volga German Republic.

Discussion of Ukrainian dialects in the German Volga republic with the text in German and Russian.

50. German Volga ASSR. Tsentral'nyi ispolnitel'nyi komitet. *Khoziaistvennoe i kul'turnoe stroitel'stvo; doklad vserossiiskomu tsentral'nomu ispolnitel'nomu komitetu i sovetu narodnykh komissarov RSFSR.* Pokrovsk, 1928.

DLC

Economic and Cultural Construction. Report of the All-Russian Central Executive Committee and Council of People's Commissars of the RSFSR.

Does not directly pertain to the Germans in Russia, but is a report on industrialization and economic growth in all parts of the Soviet Union disseminated by the German Volga ASSR.

51. German Volga ASSR. Tsentral'nyi sovet narodnogo khoziaistva. *Perspektivnyi plan promyshlennosti ASS respubliki nemtsev povolzh'ia na piatiletie 1925/26–1929/30; doklad TsSNKh III-mu s'ezdu sovetov ASSRNP i VSNKh RSFSR.* Pokrovsk: Nemgosizdat, 1926.

CSt-H

Long-Term Industrial Plan of the Autonomous Soviet Socialist Republic of Volga Germans and All-Union Council of Economy of the Russian Soviet Federated Socialist Republic.

Proposed Five-Year Plan for 1925–1930 drawn up and approved by the Third Congress of Soviets of the ASSRNP in March 1926 in Pokrovsk. Excellent source of information on economic conditions among the German settlers in the 1920s.

52.   German Volga ASSR. Verkhovnyi Sovet. *Polozhenie o vyborakh v verkhovnyi sovet ASSR nemtsev povolzh'ia.* Engel's: Nemgosizdat, 1938.
DLC
Statute of Elections to the Supreme Soviet of the Autonomous Soviet Socialist Republic of Volga Germans.

53.   German Volga ASSR. Verkhovnyi Sovet. *Stenograficheskii otchet. Sozyv 1. Sessiia 1. 1938.* Engel's: Verkhovnyi sovet ASSRNP, 1938.
DLC
Supreme Soviet Stenographic Report: First Meeting, First Session, 1938.

54.   German Volga ASSR. Verkhovnyi Sovet. *Stenograficheskii otchet. Sozyv 1. Sessiia 2. 1939.* Engel's: Verkhovnyi sovet ASSRNP, 1939.
LL
Supreme Soviet Stenographic Report: First Meeting, Second Session, 1939.

55.   German Volga ASSR. Verkhovnyi Sovet. *Stenograficheskii otchet. Sozyv 1. Sessiia 3. 1940.* Engel's: Verkhovnyi sovet ASSRNP, 1940.
LL
Supreme Soviet Stenographic Report: First Meeting, Third Session, 1940.

56.   German Volga ASSR. Verkhovnyi Sovet. *Stenograficheskii otchet. Sozyv 1. Sessiia 4. 1941.* Engel's: Verkhovnyi sovet ASSRNP, 1941.
LL
Supreme Soviet Stenographic Report: First Meeting, Fourth Session, 1941.

57.   Gernet, A. fon. *Nemetskaia koloniia strel'na pod s. peterburgom 1810–1910. (Iubileinyi listok v pamiat' stoletiia sushchestvovaniia kolonii).* St. Petersburg: Tipo-litografiia Ia. Beker i Ko., n.d.
                                                                    LL
The German Colony of Strel'na Near St. Petersburg, 1810–1910 (Anniversary Edition in Memory of the 100th Anniversary of the Founding of the Colony).

Translated from the German but translator and German title not given.

58.   Gmelin, Samuil Georg. *Puteshestvie po rossii dlia izsledovaniia trekh tsarstv estestva.* 4 vols. Translated from the German. St. Petersburg: Imperatorskaia akademiia nauk, 1771–1785.
                                                                DLC NN
Travels around Russia to Investigate Three Realms of Nature.

Gmelin was a member of the 1768–1774 expeditionary force commissioned by Catherine II to explore her realm. Volume 2 describes Gmelin's visit to the foreign communal brotherhood on the Lower Volga at Sarepta.

59.   Goikhbarg, Aleksandr Grigor'evich. *Zemlevladenie i zemlepol'zovanie poddannykh vrazhdebnykh derzhav i nemetskikh vykhodtsev.* Petrograd: Izdanie iuridicheskago knizhnago sklada "Pravo," 1915.
                                                                    DLC
Land Possession and Land Use of Subjects of Hostile Powers and of German Birth.

First edition of a work containing legislation which was enacted during World War I to restrict landholdings of subjects of Russia's wartime enemies, but which also affected the former German colonists. Contains a very brief introduction.

60.   Goikhbarg, Aleksandr Grigor'evich. *Zemlevladenie i zemlepol'zovanie poddanykh vrazhdebnykh derzhav i nemetskikh vykhodtsev. Vypusk II. Svodnyi tekst zakonov 2 fevralia i 13 dekabria 1915 g. s vstupitel'nym ocherkom.* Petrograd: Izdanie iuridicheskago knizhnago sklada "Pravo," 1916.
                                                                    DLC
Land Possession and Land Use of Subjects of Hostile Powers and of German Birth. Second Edition. Combined Text of the Laws of 2 February and 13 December 1915 with an Introductory Essay.

Goikhbarg's second edition differs from the first in that he incorporates a much longer introductory and interpretive essay.

61. Gross, E. *Avt. sots. sov. resp. nemtsev povolzh'ia.* Pokrovsk: Nemgosizdat, 1926.

CSt-H DLC NN

The Autonomous Socialist Soviet Republic of Volga Germans.

Brief history of the autonomous Volga German republic with emphasis on social, cultural, and economic conditions.

62. Grot, Iakov Karlovich. *Deiatel'nost' i perepiska Derzhavina vo vremia pugachevskogo bunta.* St. Petersburg: Tipografiia akademii nauk, 1861.

DLC

The Activity and Correspondence of Derzhavin during the Pugachev rebellion.

Brief references to Pugachev's treatment of the Volga German settlements.

63. Haller, Petr Karlovich. *Vospominaniia P. K. Gallera. (Byt nemtsevkolonistov v 60-kh godakh XIX veka).* Saratov, 1927.

DLC NN

The Memoirs of P. K. Haller (The Life of the German Colonists in the 1860s).

Reminiscences of a German settler who grew up in the colony of Eckheim in Novouzensk District, Samara Province.

64. Iustus, K. F. *Privolzhskie kolonisty. (Po povodu zakona 2-go fevr. 1915 g.).* Saratov, 1917.

The Volga German Colonists (On the Occasion of the Law of 2 February 1915).

Unverified account of the Volga colonies.

65. Kamianetskii, M. *Nimtsi i ukraina. Vidnosini nimtsiv do ukraintsiv v protiagu istorii.* Winnipeg: Ukrainian Publishing Company, 1940.

CSt-H CtY NN

Germans and the Ukraine.

Polemical account of Germans in the Ukraine in Ukrainian.

66. Kamyshinskaia okruzhnaia organizatsionnaia komissiia. *Materialy k pervomu chrezvychainomu okruzhnomu s'ezdu sovetov kamyshinskogo okruga,nizhne-volzhskogo kraia.* Kamyshin: Tipografiia kombinata, 1928.
LL
Materials for the First Special District Conference of Soviets of the Kamyshin District, Lower Volga Territory.

Limited German participation indicates former colonists were not avid backers of Soviet power in this district.

67. Kamyshinskoe uezdnoe zemskoe sobranie. *Postanovleniia kamyshin-skogo uezdnogo zemskogo sobraniia.* Saratov: Tipografiia A Stsitnik, 1867–1916.
LL
Resolutions of the Kamyshin District Zemstvo Assembly.

This was the journal of the Kamyshin District *zemstvo* assembly and board. Shows that some colonists actively participated in *zemstvo* affairs and contains interesting statistical information on the colonies.

68. Klaus, Aleksandr Avgustovich. *Nashi kolonii. Opyty materialy po istorii i statistike inostrannoi kolonizatsii v rossii.* St. Petersburg: Tipografiia V. V. Nusval't, 1869.
DLC NNC
Our Colonies: The Lessons of Materials Based on the History and Statistics of Foreign Colonization in Russia.

Written by a former colonist who later joined government service and helped administer the German colonies, this monograph is one of the best on the subject even though it has its bias and is very sketchy in some areas. In 1887 it was translated into German by J. Töws and published as *Unsere Kolonien.* It was reprinted in 1972 by Oriental Research Partners. Contemporary Russian reviews of Klaus's book can be found in these newspapers: *Golos,* no. 125 (7 May 1869): 3; *Moskovskiia vedomosti,*no. 190 (2 September 1869): 2–3, and no. 192 (4 September 1869): 2; *S. Peterburgskiia vedomosti,* no. 164 (17 June 1869): 1, and no. 168 (21 June 1869): 1.

69. Köppen, Petr. *Deviataia reviziia. Izsledovanie o chisle zhitelei v rossii v 1851 godu.* St. Petersburg: Imperatorskaia akademiia nauk, 1857.
LL
The Ninth Revision: An Investigation of the Number of Inhabitants in Russia in 1851.

A summary of the ninth revision which only gives gross population figures for the German colonists in Russia.

70. Kotov, Grigorii Grigor'evich. *Rasseianie sredne-volzhskoi derevni*. Samara: Gubernskii statisticheskii otdel, 1928.

DLC

The Dispersion of the Middle-Volga Village.

Decimation of Volga villages as a result of World War I and the Civil War.

71. Krest'ianinov, Viktor Fedorovich. *Mennonity*. Moscow: Izdatel'stvo polit. literatury, 1967.

DLC NN

The Mennonites.

Soviet work on the Mennonites of tangential relevance to the German settlers.

72. Kukhovarenko, Iu. and Barkhatov, I. *Semennaia rabota s.-kh. kooperatsii v nemrespublike. K XVIII sessii soveta sel'sko-soiuza*. Pokrovsk: Nemgosizdat, 1925.

LL

The Seed Work of the Agricultural Cooperatives in the Volga German Republic: For the Eighteenth Session of the Council of Agricultural Unions.

Technical report.

73. Kukhovarenko, Iu. and Barkhatov, I. *Semennaia rabota s.-kh. kooperatsii v nemrespublike. K XVIII sessii soveta sel'skosoiuza*. 2d rev. ed. Pokrovsk: Nemgosizdat, 1926.

LL

The Seed Work of the Agricultural Cooperatives in the Volga German Republic: For the Eighteenth Session of the Council of Agricultural Unions.

Technical report.

74. Kurts, V. A., ed. *Sarpino-tkatskaia promyshlennost' s 1921–1922 g. Otchet upravleniia tekstil'noi promyshlennosti obl. nemtsev povolzh'ia*. Pokrovsk: Nemgosizdat, 1922.

LL

The Calico Weaving Industry from 1921 to 1922: Report of the Administration of the Textile Industry of the German Volga Oblast.

75. Leopol'dov, Andrei. *Istoricheskii ocherk saratovskago kraia*. Moscow: Tipografiia S. Selivanskago, 1848.

DLC NN

Historical Sketch of Saratov Territory.

Sketchily deals with Saratov geography, economy, and government administration up to 1848. Very good for background but does not deal with colonies per se.

76. Leopol'dov, Andrei, comp. *Statisticheskoe opisanie saratovskoi gubernii*. 2 vols. in 1. St. Petersburg: Tipografiia departamenta vneshnei torgovli, 1839.

DLC

Statistical Description of Saratov Province.

A good book on early development of the province. It contains information on German colonies, including the east-bank colonies in Novouzensk District.

77. Lepekhin, Ivan Ivanovich. *Dnevnyia zapiski puteshestviia doktora i akademii nauk ad'iunkta Ivana Lepekhina po raznym provintsiiam rossiiskago gosudarstva, 1768–1772*. 4 vols. St. Petersburg: Tipografiia imperatorskoi akademii nauk, 1795–1814.

CtY DLC NN

The Daily Notes from the Travels of Doctor and Adjunct of the Academy of Sciences Ivan Lepekhin through Various Provinces of the Russian State, 1768–1772.

The traveling doctor visited the Volga provinces as part of his expedition.

78. Lindeman, Karl Eduardovich. *Prekrashchenie zemlevladeniia i zemlepol'zovaniia poselian' sobstvennikov. Ukazy 2 fevralia i 13 dekabria 1915 goda i 10, 15 iiulia i 19 avgusta 1916 goda i ikh vliianie na ekonomicheskoe sostoianie iuzhnoi rossii*. Moscow: K. L. Men'shova, 1917.

DLC

The Curtailment of Landownership and Land Use of Settler Owners. The Decrees of 2 February and 13 December 1915, and 10, 15 July and 19 August 1916, and Their Influence on the Economic Situation in Southern Russia.

Excellent monograph dealing with the wartime legislation expropriating the lands of the German settlers. Legislation arose from strong anti-German feeling in the Russian empire.

79. Lindeman, Karl Eduardovich. *Zakony 2-ogo fevralia i 13-ogo dekabria 1915 g. (Ob ogranichenii nemetskago zemlevladeniia v rossii); ikh vliianie na ekonomicheskoe sostoianie iuzhnoi rossii.* Moscow: K. L. Men'shova, 1916.

DLC

The Laws of 2 February and 13 December 1915 (about the Limitation of German Landowning in Russia) and Their Influence on the Economic Situation in Southern Russia.

Excellent work on the subject.

80. Liprandi, A. P., pseud. [Volynets, A.] *Germaniia v rossii.* Kharkov: "Mirnyi trud," 1911.

NN

Germany in Russia.

Tract against the growing German influence in the Ukraine.

81. Liprandi, A. P., pseud. [Volynets, A.]. *Kak ostanovit' mirnoe zavoevanie nashikh okrain? Nemetskii vopros, sushchnost' i znachenie ego v iugozapadnoi rossii.* Kiev: Tipografiia gen. Bruna, 1890.

CSt-H

How to Stop the Peaceful Conquest of Our Borderlands: The German Question, Its Essence and Significance in Southwestern Russia.

Typical of anti-German colonist polemics which emerged in 1890s and continued until 1917. Its focus is on Germans living in Volynia and Black Sea region.

82. Luppov, P. *Nemetskie nachal'nye shkoly v rossii. K voprosu o nemetskikh koloniiakh na russkoi zemle.* Petrograd, 1916.

LL

German Primary Schools in Russia: Concerning the Question of German Colonies on Russian Soil.

Urges closer supervision and administration of German parish schools by tsarist officials.

83.   Melitopol'skoe uezdnoe zemskoe sobranie. *Postanovleniia meli-topol'skago uezdnago zemskago sobraniia*. Melitopol: Tipografiia P. Pezeli, 1870–1916.

LL

Resolutions of the Melitopol District Zemstvo Assembly.

Official journal of the Melitopol District *zemstvo* assembly and board.

84.   Minkh, Aleksandr Nikolaevich. *Istoriko-geograficheskii slovar' sara-tovskoi gubernii*. 3 vols. Saratov: Tipografiia gubernskago zemstva, 1898–1901.

DLC

Historical-Geographic Dictionary of Saratov Province.

A very detailed encyclopedia on Saratov Province, where many Volga Germans settled. Alphabetically arranged with extensive articles on the history and geography of the province. Excellent maps included.

85.   Murav'ev, M. V., ed. *"Nemetskoe zlo" sbornik statei posviashchennykh voprosu o bor'be s nashei "vnutrennei germaniei."* Moscow: Tipografiia A. I. Mamontov, 1915.

CSt-H NN

"The German Evil": A Collection of Articles Devoted to the Question of the Struggle with Our "Internal Germany."

World War I anti-German literature without footnotes and with few references to sources.

86.   Mysh, Mikhail Ignat'evich, ed. *Ob inostranntsakh v rossii. Sbornik uzakonenii, traktatov i konventsii, s otnosiashchimisia k nim pravitel'stvennym i sudebnymi raz'iasneniiami*. 2d rev. ed. St. Petersburg: Tipografiia A. Benke, 1911.

DLC

Concerning Foreigners in Russia: A Collection of Statutes, Tracts, and Conventions with Government and Legal Interpretations Pertaining to Them.

Very valuable work which contains a section on the changing legal status of the German colonies, especially after the 1860 reforms.

87.   Nabatov, Grigorii I. *Respublika bez mezhei: respublika nemtsev povolzh'ia*. Moscow: Priboi, 1930.

NN

Republic without Borders: The Republic of Volga Germans.

Propaganda piece addressed to all nationalities in the Soviet Union.

88.   Nikolaevskoe uezdnoe zemskoe sobranie. *Postanovleniia nikolaev-skogo uezdnogo zemskogo sobraniia.* Samara: Zemskaia tipografiia, 1868–1916.

LL

Resolutions of the Nikolaev District Zemstvo Assembly.

Official journal of the Nikolaev District, Samara Province, *zemstvo* assembly and board. A significant number of Volga Germans lived in Nikolaev District.

89.   Novouzenskoe uezdnoe zemskoe sobranie. *Zhurnaly novouzenskogo uezdnogo zemskogo sobraniia.* Saratov: Tipografiia saratovskogo spravoch-nogo listka, 1868–1916.

LL

Journals of the Novouzensk District Zemstvo Assembly.

Official accounts of the Novouzensk District *zemstvo* assembly.

90.   Novouzenskoe uezdnoe zemstvo. *Novouzenskii uezd v estestvenno-istoricheskom i khoziaistvennom otnoshenii. Po dannym obsledovanniia 1908 g.* 2 vols. Novouzensk: Tipografiia obshchestva trudovoi pomoshchi, 1912, 1913.

LL

Natural-Historical and Economic Aspects of Novouzensk District, Based on Information from the Inspection of 1908.

A superlative *zemstvo* publication covering all aspects of Novouzensk District, which contained largest number of Volga Germans. Plethora of statistical information and maps. Gives *volost*-level information on households, landownership, livestock holdings, sex-ratio, and many other topics.

91.   Obolenskii, Valerian V., pseud. [Osinskii]. *Mezhdunarodnye i mezhkontinental'nye migratsii v dovoennoi rossii i SSSR.* Moscow: Tsent-ral'noe statisticheskoe upravlenie SSSR, 1928.

CSt-H DLC

International and Intercontinental Migration in Prewar Russia and Soviet Union.

Carefully researched and statistically full account of immigration to and emigration from Russia. Discusses migrations of the German settlers.

92. *Otchet nemetsko-volzhskogo banka s.-kh. kredita za vremia s 1 oktiabria 1923 g. po 30 sentiabria 1924 g.* Pokrovsk: Izdatel'stvo Nemvolbanka, 1925.

Unverified

Report of the Volga German Bank of Agricultural Credit for the Period 1 October 1923 to 30 September 1924.

Unverified pamphlet on the Volga German Bank of Agricultural Credit.

93. Padalka, Lev Vasil'evich. *Zemlevladenie nemtsev, byvshikh kolonistov v khersonskoi gubernii.* Kherson: Izdanie khersonskoe gubernskoe zemstvo, 1891.

DLC

Landownership of the Germans, Former Colonists in Kherson Province.

A short but more balanced account of German landowning which appeared in the late nineteenth century.

94. Pallas, Peter Simon. *Kratkoe fizicheskoe i topograficheskoe opisanie tavricheskoi oblasti.* St. Petersburg: Imperatorskaia tipografiia moskovskago universiteta, 1795.

DLC NN

A Short Physical and Topographical Description of the Tauride Region.

Physical description of Tauride Province drawn from Pallas's participation in an expedition commissioned by Catherine II.

95. Patkanov, S. K. *Itogi statistiki immigratsii v soedinnenye shtaty sev. ameriki iz rossii za desiatiletie 1900–1909 g.g.* St. Petersburg: Tipo-litografiia N. L. Nyrkina, 1911.

CSt-H

Statistical Results of Immigration from Russia to the United States of North America for the Ten-Year Period 1900–1909.

Excellent work for comparative approach to study of various nationalities immigrating to the United States from Russia. Based on extensive statistics.

96. Pavlovskii, I. F. *Nemetskiia kolonii v poltavskoi gubernii v XIX st. (1808–1867). (Po arkhivnym dannym). (Ottisk s 10-go vypuska trudov poltavskoi uchenoi arkhivnoi komissii).* Poltava: Tipografiia G. I. Markevicha, 1913.

LL

German Colonies in Poltava Province in the 19th Century (1808–1867). (Based on Archival Information). (Reprint from the Tenth Number of the Works of the Poltava Scientific Archival Committee).

Explores settlement of Germans in Poltava, Kremenchug, and Konstantinograd in Poltava Province beginning in 1809. Describes home construction, arrival, and gives names of first group of 130 in August, 1809. A very valuable book on these little known colonies.

97.   Peretiatkovich, Georgii Ivanovich. *Povolzh'e v XV i XVI vekakh. (Ocherki iz istorii kraia i ego kolonizatsii)*. Moscow: Grachevo, 1877.
DLC
The Volga Region in the Fifteenth and Sixteenth Centuries: Essays on the History of the Region and Its Colonization.

Detailed account of the Volga region before the arrival of the foreign settlers.

98.   Peretiatkovich, Georgii Ivanovich. *Povolzh'e v XVII i nachale XVIII veka. (Ocherki iz istorii kolonizatsii kraia)* Odessa: P. A. Zelenago, 1882.
DLC
The Volga Region in the Seventeenth and Beginning of the Eighteenth Centuries: Essays on the History of Colonization of the Region.

This sequel to Peretiatkovich's earlier tome brings the history of the Volga region down to the time of the arrival of the first foreign colonists in the years 1763–1764.

99.   Pershin, Pavel Nikolaevich. *Uchastkovoe zemlepol'zovanie v rossii. Khutora i otruba, ikh rasprostranenie za desiatiletie 1907–1916 gg. i sudby vo vremia revoliutsii 1917–1920 gg.* Moscow: Izdatel'stvo Narkomzema "Novaia derevnia," 1922.
NN
Private Land Use in Russia: Khutora and Otruba, Their Diffusion for the Decade 1907–1916, and Their Fate during the Revolution, 1917–1920.

100.   Pisarevskii, Grigorii Grigor'evich. *Iz istorii inostrannoi kolonizatsii v rossii v XVIII v. (Po neizdannym arkhivnym dokumentam)*. Moscow: Pechatnia A. I. Snegirevyi, 1909.
CtY NN

History of Foreign Colonization in Russia in the Eighteenth Century (Based on Unpublished Archive Documents).

Best account in any language of settlement of foreign colonies. Serialized in *Russkii vestnik* 253, no. 1; 255, no. 6; 259, no. 1; 266, no. 3.

101. Pisarevskii, Grigorii Grigor'evich. *Khoziaistvo i forma zemlevladeniia v koloniiakh povolzh'ia v XVIII-m i v pervoi chetverti XIX-go veka*. Rostov-on-Don: Tipografiia A. I. Ter-Abramian, 1916.

LL

The Farm and Form of Landownership in the Colonies of the Volga in the Eighteenth and First Quarter of the Nineteenth Centuries.

The problems and land arrangements of the Volga colonies as presented by the leading Russian scholar on the history of the Volga Germans.

102. Pisarevskii, Grigorii Grigor'evich. *K istorii iezuitov v rossii (veroispovednyi vopros v koloniiakh povolzh'ia sto let tomu nazad)*. Warsaw: Tipografiia varshavskago uchebnago okruga, 1912.

LL

Concerning the History of the Jesuits in Russia: The Religious Question in the Volga Colonies One Hundred Years Ago.

Deals with the problem of supplying qualified clergy to the Catholic Volga colonies.

103. Pisarevskii, Grigorii Grigor'evich. *Pereselenie prusskikh mennonitov v rossiiu pri Aleksandre I*. Rostov-on-Don: Tipografiia S. S. Sivozhelezov, 1917.

NN

The Settlement of Prussian Mennonites in Russia during the Reign of Alexander I.

Deals with Mennonite settlement in New Russia.

104. Pisarevskii, Grigorii Grigor'evich. *Vnutrennii rasporiadok v koloniiakh povolzh'ia pri Ekaterine II*. Warsaw: Tipografiia varshavskago uchebnago okruga, 1914.

NN

Internal Order in the Volga Colonies during the Reign of Catherine II.

Brief but very good account of the internal administration of the Volga colonies which was also published in *Varshavskiia universitetskiia izves-tiia*. See also entry 302.

105.   *Polozhenie sel'skogo khoziaistva obl. nemtsev povolzh'ia po dannym podvornogo obsledovaniia na 1-e ianv. 1922 g.* Marxstadt: Izdatel'stvo Obze-mupravleniia, 1922.

LL

The Condition of Agricuture in the Volga German Oblast according to Figures Based on Household Inspections on 1 January 1922.

Reveals to what extent Volga German agriculture had deteriorated as a result of World War I and the Civil War.

106.   Pototskii, Stepan Vasil'evich. *Inzov, Ivan Nikitich, general-ot-infan-terii, glavnyi popechitel' i predsedatel' popechitel'nago komiteta ob inostrannykh poselentsakh iuzhnago kraia rossii. Biograficheskii ocherk.* Bendery: Tipo-grafiia E. Natenzon-Postan, 1904.

CU

Ivan Nikitich Inzov: Infantry General, Chief Trustee and Chairman of the Guardianship Committee of the Foreign Settlements in the Southern Region of Russia: A Biographical Sketch.

Biography of one of the tsarist bureaucrats responsible for the southern colonists.

107.   Pototskii, Stepan Vasil'evich. *Istoriko-geograficheskii ocherk bes-sarabskoi gubernii.* Yalta: Tipografiia N. V. Vakhtina, 1902.

LL

An Historical-Geographical Essay on the Province of Bessarabia.

108.   Rennikov, A. M. *Zoloto reina o nemtsakh v rossii.* Petrograd: Tipografiia T-va A. S. Suvorin, 1915.

CSt-H NN

The Gold of the Rhine: Concerning the Germans in Russia.

Polemical attack on German Black Sea settlers with no claim to scholar-liness except for some maps of colonial settlement.

109.   Russia. Laws, statutes, etc. *Polnoe sobranie zakonov rossiiskoi imperii. Sobranie pervoe. S 1649–12 dek. 1825.* 44 vols. in 51. St. Petersburg, 1830.

CSt-H CtY CU DLC NN NNC

The Complete Collection of Laws of the Russian Empire. First Edition. From 1649 to 12 December 1825.

The texts of more than 30,600 legislative enactments beginning with the Code of 1649 and ending with the reign of Alexander I on 12 December 1825.

110.   Russia. Laws, statutes, etc. *Polnoe sobranie zakonov rossiiskoi imperii. Sobranie vtoroe. S 12 dekabria 1825–1881.* 40 vols. in 125. St. Petersburg, 1830–1884.

CSt-H CtY CU DLC NN NNC

The Complete Collection of Laws of the Russian Empire. Second Edition. From 12 December 1825 to 1881.

Legislation enacted during the reigns of Nicholas I and Alexander II.

111.   Russia. Laws, statutes, etc. *Polnoe sobranie zakonov rossiiskoi imperii. Sobranie tret'e. 1 marta 1881–1913.* 33 vols. in 49. St. Petersburg, 1885–1916.

CSt-H CtY CU DLC NN NNC

The Complete Collection of Laws of the Russian Empire. Third Edition. From 1 March 1881 to 1913.

Legislation enacted for the period March 1881–1913, when publication was terminated by the revolution.

112.   Russia. Laws, statutes, etc. *Svod zakonov rossiiskoi imperii (izdaniia 1857 goda).* Vol. 12, pt. 2, bk. 4: "Svod uchrezhdenii i ustavov o koloniiakh inostrantsev v imperii," pp. 3–100.

DLC

Code of Laws of the Russian Empire, 1857 Edition. "Code of Institutions and Statutes Relating to the Foreign Colonists in the Empire."

Essential legal code which defined the legal status of the colonists.

113.   Russia. Laws, statutes, etc. *Svod zakonov rossiiskoi imperii (izdaniia 1902).* Vol. 9. "Osoboe prilozhenie k zakonam o sostoianiikh, polozheniia o sel'skom sostoianii," pp. 1–791.

DLC

Code of Laws of the Russian Empire, 1902 Edition. "Special Supplement to Laws regarding [Legal] Status, Statutes regarding Agricultural Conditions."

Laws which applied to the former colonists and dealt with governmental administration, landholding, and legal status within the empire.

114.   Russia. Ministerstvo finansov. *Otchet po izsledovanniiu volzhskoi khlebnoi torgovli, proizvedennomu po poruchenniiu ministerstva finansov i gosudarstvennykh imushchestv v 1886 g. A. A. Klopovym.* St. Petersburg: Tipografiia V. Kirshbauma, 1887.

					DLC

Investigative Report on the Volga Grain Trade Prepared on the Orders of the Ministry of Finance and State Domains in 1886 by A. A. Klopov.

Provides statistical information on Volga German wheat production and shipment to other areas of Russia.

115.   Russia. Ministerstvo finansov. *Otchet po izsledovanniiu volzhskoi khlebnoi torgovli, proizvedennomu po poruchenniiu ministerstva finansov i gosudarstvennykh imushchestv v 1887 g. A. A. Klopovym.* St. Petersburg: Tipografiia V. Kirshbauma, 1889.

					DLC

Investigative Report on the Volga Grain Trade Prepared on the Orders of the Ministry of Finance and State Domains in 1887 by A. A. Klopov.

See comments on entry 114.

116.   Russia. Ministerstvo finansov. *Otchet po izsledovanniiu volzhskoi khlebnoi torgovli, proizvedennomu po porucheniiu ministerstva finansov v 1888 i 1889 g. g. A. A. Klopovym.* Tver: Tipografiia gubernskago pravleniia, 1889.

					DLC

Investigative Report on the Volga Grain Trade Prepared on the Orders of the Ministry of Finance in 1888 and 1889 by A. A. Klopov.

See comments on entry 114.

117.   Russia. Ministerstvo gosudarstvennykh imushchestv. *Obozrenie deiatel'nosti ministerstva gosudarstvennykh imushchestv po zavedyvanniiu gosudarstvennymi krest'ianami i iuzhnymi poselianami s 1838 po 1866 god.* St. Petersburg: Tipografiia V. Bezobrazova, 1867.

					LL

A Review of the Activity of the Ministry of State Domains in the Management of State Peasants and Southern Settlers from 1838 to 1866.

Official account of government management of German settlements in New Russia.

118. Russia. Ministerstvo gosudarstvennykh imushchestv. *Statisticheskii obzor gosudarstvennykh imushchestv za 1858 god.* St. Petersburg: Tipografiia ministerstva gosudarstvennykh imushchestv, 1861.

DLC

Statistical Review of State Domains for the Year 1858.

A general statistical review of all state domains; includes general land figures on the foreign settlements.

119. Russia. Tsentral'nyi statisticheskii komitet. *Goroda i poseleniia v uezdakh imeiushchie 2000 i bolee zhitelei.* St. Petersburg: Tipografiia N. L. Nyrkina, 1905.

CtY DLC NN

Towns and Settlements in Districts Having 2,000 or More Inhabitants.

Census of towns and villages with at least 2,000 residents.

120. Russia. Tsentral'nyi statisticheskii komitet. *Pervaia vseobshchaia perepis' naseleniia rossiiskoi imperii, 1897 g.* Edited by N. A. Troinitskii. 89 vols. in 24. St. Petersburg: Izdatel'stvo tsentral'nago statisticheskago komiteta ministerstva vnutrennikh del, 1899–1900.

CtY DLC NN

The First General Census of the Population of the Russian Empire, 1897.

The only general population census taken during the tsarist period. Provides data on German settlers on such topics as age, nationality, literacy, occupation, marital status, and religion.

121. Russia. Tsentral'nyi statisticheskii komitet. *Spiski naselennykh mest rossiiskoi imperii, sostavlennye i izdavaemye tsentral'nym statisticheskim komitetom ministerstva vnutrennikh del. (Po svedeniiam 1859).* 47 vols. in 42. St. Petersburg: Tipografiia Karl Vul'f, 1861–1885.

DLC NN

Vol. 3—Bessarabskaia oblast', 1861.
Vol. 12—Zemlia donskogo voiska, 1864.
Vol. 13—Ekaterinoslavskaia guberniia, 1863.
Vol. 33—Poltavskaia guberniia, 1862.
Vol. 36—Samarskaia guberniia, 1864.
Vol. 38—Saratovskaia guberniia, 1862.
Vol. 39—Simbirskaia guberniia, 1863.
Vol. 41—Tavricheskaia guberniia, 1865.
Vol. 46—Khar'kovskaia guberniia, 1869.
Vol. 47—Khersonskaia guberniia, 1868.

Lists of Populated Places of the Russian Empire, Compiled and Published by the Central Statistical Committee of the Ministry of Internal Affairs (Based on 1859 Data).

Vol. 3—Bessarabia Region, 1861.
Vol. 12—The Land of the Don Forces, 1864.
Vol. 13—Ekaterinoslav Province, 1863.
Vol. 33—Poltava Province, 1862.
Vol. 36—Samara Province, 1864.
Vol. 38—Saratov Province, 1862.
Vol. 39—Simbirsk Province, 1863.
Vol. 41—Tauride Province, 1865.
Vol. 46—Kharkov Province, 1869.
Vol. 47—Kherson Province, 1868.

Includes very useful demographic data on the forty-three provinces of European Russia. All have introductions on the people, land, and economy. Numerous scaled maps.

122.   Russia (1923–USSR) Tsentral'noe statisticheskoe upravlenie. Otdel perepisi. *Vsesoiuznaia perepis' naseleniia 1926 goda.* 57 vols. in 49. Moscow: Tsentral'noe Statisticheskoe upravlenie, 1928–1933.

                                                              CtY DLC
The 1926 General Census of the Population.

First complete census of the population of the Soviet Union. Data includes information on age, sex, nationality, mother tongue, literacy, occupation, marital status, place of birth, length of residence, unemployment, and structure of the urban family.

123.   Russia (1923–USSR). Tsentral'nyi ispolnitel'nyi komitet. *O sovetskom, khoziaistvennom i kul'turnom stroitel'stve ASSR nemtsev povolzh'ia; postanovlenie.* Engel's: Nemgosizdat, 1936.

                                                              DLC
Concerning Soviet, Economic, and Cultural Construction in the Autonomous Republic of Volga Germans: Resolutions.

124.   Samara, Russia (Government). Gubernskaia komissiia pomoshchi golodaiushchim. *Kniga o golode. Ekonomicheskii, bytovoi, literaturno-khudozhestvennyi sbornik.* Samara: Gos. izdatel'stvo, samarskoe otdelenie, 1922.

                                                              CSt-H

The Book on Famine: Collection of Articles on the Economy, Conditions of Daily Life, Literature, and Art.

A collection of articles dealing with the harsh famine of 1921–1922 which seriously affected the Volga Germans.

125. Samara, Russia (Government). Gubernskaia komissiia pomoshchi golodaiushchim. *Na fronte goloda.* Samara: Gos. izdatel'stvo, smarskoe otdelenie, 1922.

CSt-H

On the Famine Front.

Describes the disastrous 1921–1922 famine in the Volga valley.

126. Samara, Russia (Government). Gubernskii statisticheskii otdel. *Naselenie samarskoi gubernii po dannym vsesoiuznoi perepisi 17 dekabria 1926 g.* Samara: Gubernskii statisticheskii otdel, 1928.

DLC

The Population of Samara Province Based on Data from the General Census of 17 December 1926.

127. Samara, Russia (Government). Gubernskoe statisticheskoe biuro. *Chislennost' sel'skogo naseleniia v samarskoi gubernii.* 2d ed. Samara: Tip. no. 4 sovnarkhoza, 1920.

CSt-H DLC

The Size of Rural Population of Samara Province.

Very brief and general enumeration of the rural population of Samara Province which included a number of former colonists.

128. Samara, Russia (Government). Gubernskoe statisticheskoe biuro. *Sel'sko-khoziaistvennyi obzor samarskoi gubernii za 1915 god.* 2d rev. ed. Samara: Tip. politodarma iuzhgruppy vostfronta, 1919.

CSt-H

An Agricultural Survey of Samara Province for 1915.

This survey presents production figures but does not differentiate producers, so it is impossible to discern production figures for German settlers.

129. Samarskaia gubernskaia zemskaia uprava. Otsenochnostatisticheskoe otdelenie. *Materialy po otsenke-zemel' nikolaevskogo uezda. Krest'ianskoe khoziaistvo.* Samara: Zemskaia tipografiia, 1904.

LL

Materials for an Evaluation of the Land of Nikolaevsk District. Peasant Farming.

Provides information on soil conditions, crops, terrain, and methods of agriculture in this Volga German populated district.

130.   Samarskii gubernskii statisticheskii komitet. *Pamiatnaia knizhka samarskoi gubernii za 1863–1864 g.* Samara: Gubernskaia tipografiia, 1864.
LL
Memorandum Book of Samara Province for 1863–1864.

Review of the major events occurring in Samara Province during 1863–1864.

131.   Samarskii gubernskii statisticheskii otdel. *Spisok naselennykh punktov samarskoi gubernii.* Edited by G. Kotov. Samara: Samizdattorg, 1928.
LL
A List of Populated Places in Samara Province.

132.   Saratov, Russia (Government). Gubernskaia zemskaia uprava. Otsenochno–statisticheskoe otdelenie. *Spiski naselennykh mest saratovskoi gubernii.* Saratov: Zemskaia tipografiia, 1912.
NNC
Lists of Populated Places of Saratov Province.

Reports *volost*-level figures on population, landholding, livestock holdings, and equipment ownership in Saratov Province in 1911. Also has very good maps.

133.   Saratov, Russia (Government). Gubernskoe statisticheskoe biuro. *Statisticheskii sbornik po saratovskoi gubernii.* Saratov: Sarnoligrafprom. Tip. No. 11, 1923.
CSt-H
A Statistical Collection on Saratov Province.

Economic and demographic statistics of Saratov Province in 1922.

134.   Saratov, Russia (Government). Gubernskoe statisticheskoe biuro. *Tablitsy statisticheskikh svedenii po saratovskoi gubernii po dannym vserossiiskoi sel'sko-khoziaistvennoi i gorodskoi perepisei 1917 goda. (Itogi predvari-*

tel'nago podscheta). Saratov: Tipografiia No. 7 soveta nar. khoz., 1919.

NcD

Tables of Statistical Information on Saratov Province Based on Data from the All-Russian Agricultural and City Census of 1917: Results of a Preliminary Calculation.

Detailed report on agriculture and economy in Saratov Province. Broken down by district and *volost*. Statistics on landholding, population, livestock, grain production, and many other topics. Based on the 1917 census.

135. Saratovskaia gubernskaia zemskaia uprava. *Materialy o sostoianii narodnogo obrazovaniia v saratovskoi gubernii za 1910–1911 god*. Saratov: Tipografiia gubernskoe zemstvo, 1916.

LL

Materials on the Condition of Public Education in Saratov Province for 1910–1911.

A history of education in Saratov Province which discusses the vital role of education in the Volga colonies and presents a chart listing founding dates of German schools.

136. Saratovskaia uchenaia arkhivnaia komissiia. *Saratovskii istoricheskii sbornik*. 1 vol. Saratov: Tipografiia gubernskago zemstva, 1891.

LL

Saratov Historical Collection.

Only one volume of this historical collection was ever published. This volume is the diary of Gerasim Alekseevich Skopin (1746–1797), an Orthodox religious leader who served most of his life in the Lower Volga valley.

137. Saratovskaia uchenaia arkhivnaia komissiia. *Trudy saratovskoi uchenoi arkhivnoi komissii*. Saratov: Tipografiia gubernskago zemstva, 1888–1923.

LL NN

Works of the Saratov Scientific Archival Committee.

A scholarly serial publication on the history, ethnography, and geography of Saratov Province. Irregular numbering of volumes. New York Public Library has volumes 24–31, 33 (1908–1916). Articles appearing in the *Trudy* relating to the Volga German settlers are listed separately in the section on articles and statutes in this bibliography.

138. *Sbornik statisticheskikh svedenii o poltavskoi gubernii*.Poltava: Poltavskii gubernskii statisticheskii komitet, 1869.
LL
Collection of Statistical Information on Poltava Province.

This abundantly rich *zemstvo* publication contains data on various aspects of provincial life in Poltava, as well as a history of the region.

139. *Sbornik statisticheskikh svedenii po avtonomnoi sotsialisticheskikh sovetskoi respubliki nemtsev povolzh'ia. 1916–1924 gg.* Pokrovsk: Tsentral'noe statisticheskoe upravlenie ASSRNP, 1924.
LL
Collection of Statistical Information on the Autonomous Soviet Socialist Republic of Volga Germans. 1916–1924.

Essential statistical source on the Volga Germans.

140. *Sbornik statisticheskikh svedenii po ekaterinoslavskii gubernii.* 3 vols. Ekaterinoslav: Ekaterinoslavskoe gubernskoe zemstvo, 1884–1886.
LL
Vol. 1—Rostovskii na-donu uezd i taganrogskoe gradonachal'stvo, 1884.
Vol. 2—Bakhmutskii uezd, 1886.
Vol. 3—Slavianoserbskii uezd, 1886.

Collection of Statistical Information on Ekaterinoslav Province.

Vol. 1—Rostov-on-Don District and the Town of Taganrog, 1884.
Vol. 2—Bakhmut District, 1886.
Vol. 3—Slavianoserb District, 1886.

141. *Sbornik statisticheskikh svedenii po samarskoi gubernii.* 8 vols. Moscow and Samara: Samarskoe gubernskoe zemstvo, 1883–1892.
LL
Vol. 1—Samarskii uezd, 1883.
Vol. 2—Stavropol'skii uezd, 1884.
Vol. 3—Bugulukskii uezd, 1885.
Vol. 4—Buguruslanskii uezd, 1886.
Vol. 5—Bugul'minskii uezd, 1887.
Vol. 6—Nikolaevskii uezd, 1889.
Vol. 7—Novouzenskii uezd, 1890.
Vol. 8—Samarskaia guberniia, 1892.

Collection of Statistical Information on Samara Province.

Vol. 1—Samara District, 1883.
Vol. 2—Stavropol District, 1884.
Vol. 3—Buguluk District, 1885.
Vol. 4—Buguruslan District, 1886.
Vol. 5—Bugul'min District, 1887.
Vol. 6—Nikolaev District, 1889.
Vol. 7—Novouzensk District, 1890.
Vol. 8—Samara Province, 1892.

Innumerable statistical data on the Volga German settlers.

142. *Sbornik statisticheskikh svedenii po saratovskoi gubernii*. 12 vols. Saratov: Saratovskoe gubernskoe zemstvo, 1883–1897.

LL

Vol. 1—Saratovskii uezd, 1883.
Vol. 2—Tsaritsyn uezd, 1884.
Vol. 3—Saratovskii & Tsaritsyn uezd, 1884.
Vol. 4—Petrovsk & Atkarsk uezd, 1884.
Vol. 5—Khvalynskii uezd, 1886.
Vol. 6—Atkarsk uezd: no. 1 (1887); no. 2 (1896).
Vol. 7—Vol'zhskii uezd: no. 1 (1897); no. 2 (1892).
Vol. 8—Tablitsy, 1888.
Vol. 9—Serdobskii uezd, 1892.
Vol. 10—Kuznetskii uezd, 1891.
Vol. 11—Kamyshinskii uezd, 1891.
Vol. 12—Balashovskii uezd: no. 1 (1893); no. 2 (1897).

Statistical Information on Saratov Province.

Vol. 1—Saratov District, 1883.
Vol. 2—Tsaritsyn District, 1884.
Vol. 3—Saratov and Tsaritsyn District, 1884.
Vol. 4—Petrovsk and Atkarsk District, 1884.
Vol. 5—Khvalyn District, 1886.
Vol. 6—Atkarsk District, 1887, 1896.
Vol. 7—Volga District, 1897, 1892.
Vol. 8—Tables, 1888.
Vol. 9—Serdobol District, 1892.
Vol. 10—Kuznetsk District, 1891.
Vol. 11—Kamyshin District, 1891.
Vol. 12—Balashov District, 1893, 1897.

Contains significant information on the Volga colonies in Saratov Province.

143.   *Sbornik statisticheskikh svedenii po tavricheskoi gubernii*. 9 vols. Simferopol: Tavricheskoe gubernskoe zemstvo, 1885–1889.

LL

Vol. 1—Melitopol'skii uezd: no. 1 (1885); no. 2 (1887).
Vol. 2—Dneprovskii uezd, 1886.
Vol. 3—Feodosiiskii uezd & Kerch-Enikal'skoe
gradonachal'stvo, 1886.
Vol. 4—Simferopol'skii uezd, 1886.
Vol. 5—Berdianskii uezd, 1887.
Vol. 6—Perekopskii uezd, 1887.
Vol. 7—Evpatoriiskii uezd, 1887.
Vol. 8—Ialtinskii uezd, 1887.
Vol. 9—Pamiatnaia knizhka tavricheskoi gubernii, 1889.

Collection of Statistical Information on Tauride Province.

Vol. 1—Melitopol District, 1885, 1887.
Vol. 2—Dneprovsk District, 1886.
Vol. 3—Feodosiia District and the Town of Kerch-Enikale, 1886.
Vol. 4—Simferopol District, 1886.
Vol. 5—Berdiansk District, 1887.
Vol. 6—Perekop District, 1887.
Vol. 7—Evpatoriia District, 1887.
Vol. 8—Yalta District, 1887.
Vol. 9—Memorandum Book of Tauride Province, 1889.

Many Black Sea Germans lived in these districts. Considerable attention is devoted to them in these *zemstvo* publications.

144.   *Sel'sko-khoziaistvennaia kooperatsiia ASSR nemtsev povolzh'ia. (Materialy po dokladu pravleniia nemsel'skosoiuza na XVIII sessii soveta sel'skosoiuza)*. Pokrovsk: Nemgosizdat, 1925.

LL

Agricultural Cooperatives in the Volga German Republic (Materials according to the Report of the Administration of the German Agricultural Unions for the Eighteenth Session of the Council of Agricultural Unions).

145.   Semenov-Tian-Shanskii, Petr P., ed. *Geografichesko-statisticheskii slovar' rossiiskoi imperii*. 5 vols. St. Petersburg: Tipografiia V. Bezobrazova, 1863–1885.

CSt-H DLC NN

Geographic-Statistical Dictionary of the Russian Empire.

One of the best geographical and historical references on mid-nineteenth century Russian towns, districts, regions, and settlements.

146. Semenov-Tian-Shanskii, Petr P., ed. *Rossiia. Polnoe geograficheskoe opisanie nashego otechestva*. Vol. 14, *Novorossiia i krym*. St. Petersburg: Izdanie A. F. Devriena, 1910.

CSt-H DLC NN

Russia: A Complete Geographical Description of Our Fatherland. Vol. 14, New Russia and Crimea.

Detailed accounts of the economy, geography, and peoples of the northern Black Sea coast.

147. Semenov-Tian-Shanskii, Petr P., ed. *Rossiia. Polnoe geograficheskoe opisanie nashego otechestva*. Vol. 6, *Srednee i nizhnee povolzh'e i zavolzh'e*. St. Petersburg: Izdanie A. F. Devriena, 1901.

CSt-H DLC NN

A Complete Geographical Description of Our Fatherland. Vol. 6, The Middle and Lower Volga and Trans-Volga Region.

Detailed accounts of the economy, geography, and peoples of the Volga region.

148. Semenov-Tian-Shanskii, Veniamin Petrovich, ed. *Povolzh'e priroda, byt, khoziaistvo po volge, oke, kame, viatke i beloi*. Leningrad: Tipografiia transpechati NKPS, 1925.

DLC

The Volga Region, Nature, Daily Life, and Society along the Volga, Oka, Kama, Viatka, and Belaia Rivers.

149. Semevskii, Vasilii Ivanovich. *Krest'ianskii vopros v rossii v XVIII i pervoi polovine XIX veka*. 2 vols. St. Petersburg: Tipografiia tovarishchestva "Obshchestvennaia pol'za," 1888.

CU CtY DLC NN

The Peasant Problem in Russia in the Eighteenth and First Half of the Nineteenth Centuries.

The best study of serfdom and agrarian conditions in post-Petrine Russia.

150. Serebriakov, F. O. *Nemetskaia kommuna na volge i vozrozhdenie iugo-vostoka rossii*. Moscow, 1922.

LL

The German Commune on the Volga and the Revival of Southeastern Russia.

Narrates the history of the establishment of soviets in the Volga colonies.

151.   Sergeev, Ivan Ivanovich. *Mirnoe zavoevanie rossii nemtsami (doklad, prochitannyi v chrezvychainom obshchem sobranii g. g. chlenov "Obshchestva 1914 goda" 13 marta 1915 goda)*. Petrograd: Tipo-litografiia N. I. Evstifeev, 1915.

CSt-H NN

The Peaceful Conquest of Russia by the Germans (A Report Read at the Special General Meeting of the Distinguished Members of the "Society of 1914" on 13 March 1915).

Extremely vitriolic attack on the Germans in Russia.

152.   Shafranov, Petr A., comp. *Arkhiv ministerstva zemledeliia i gosudarstvennykh imushchestv (istoricheskii ocherk ustroistva i sostav del)*. St. Petersburg: Tipografiia V. F. Kirshbauma, 1904.

NN

The Archives of the Ministry of Agriculture and State Domains (A Historical Essay of the Arrangement and Composition of the Records).

Useful guide to records kept on the foreign settlements by the ministry in charge of them.

153.   Shafranov, Petr A. *Otzyv o knige G. G. Pisarevskogo: "Iz istorii inostrannoi kolonizatsii v rossii v XVIII veke"*. Moscow: Obshchestvo istorii i drevnostei rossii pri mosk. institute, 1909.

LL

A Review of G. G. Pisarevskii's Book: "History of Foreign Colonization in Russia in the Eighteenth Century."

Scholarly critique of Pisarevskii's doctoral dissertation (which was being considered for the Karpov Prize) by an official of long-standing in the Ministry of Agriculture and State Domains.

154.   Shamshin, Ivan Fedorovich. *Zapiska po voprosam osobago nastavleniia revisuiushchim senatoram*. 3 nos. N. p. [1881].

LL

Notes on Questions of the Special Instructions of the Senate Inspectors.

Three reports on the Senate inspection of Saratov and Samara Provinces, 1880–1881.

155. Shelukhin, Sergei. *Nemetskaia kolonizatsiia na iuge rossii*. Odessa: Tip. aktsionernago iuzhno-russkago o-va pechatnago dela, 1915.

CSt-H

German Colonization in Southern Russia.

Written by an anti-German member of the Odessa District Court, this short work has scholarly merit, especially in regard to the German settlers in Kherson Province.

156. Shevchenko, M. A. *Nizhnee povolzh'e*. Moscow-Leningrad: Gosudarstvennoe izdatel'stvo, 1929.

CSt-H

The Lower Volga Region.

Monograph on the economy, history and peoples of the Nizhne-Volzhskaia Oblast, a territorial-administrative unit formed on 1 October 1928 out of the provinces of Astrakhan and Saratov, and the Autonomous Soviet Socialist Republic of Volga Germans and the Kalmyk Autonomous Oblast. Has an excellent bibliography.

157. Shishmarev, Vladimir F. *Romanskie poseleniia na iuge rossii*. Leningrad: Izdatel'stvo "Nauka," 1975.

DLC

Romanic Settlements in Southern Russia.

Very scholarly Soviet monograph on Romance language settlers in southern Russia based on rare sources and archives. Written by a man who dedicated his entire career to the subject.

158. Shtakh, Ia. *Ocherki iz istorii i sovremennoi zhizni iuzhno-russkikh kolonistov*. Moscow: A. I. Mamontov, 1916.

NN

Essays on the History and Contemporary Life of the South-Russian Colonists.

One of the best accounts of life among the Black Sea Germans.

159. Shtrandt, L. *Kad vedut svoe khoziaistvo nemtsy povolzh'ia*. Edited by D. Shmidt. Moscow-Leningrad: GIZ, 1926.

LL

How the Volga Germans Conduct Their Agriculture.

Reports the recovery of agriculture in the Volga communities after the Civil War and famines of the early 1920s.

160.   Simbirskii, N. *Svoboda na zemle (Druz'ia i vragi russkago zemledel'tsa)*. St. Petersburg: Tipografiia "Ulei," 1912.

CSt-H

Freedom on the Land: Friends and Enemies of Russian Farmers.

Attack on all foreign ownership of Russian lands.

161.   Sinner, Peter. *Nemtsy nizhnego povolzh'ia; istoricheskii ocherk vydaiushchiesia deiateli iz kolonii povolzh'ia*. Saratov, 1925.

DLC

The Germans of the Lower Volga Region: A Historical Essay about Prominent Men from the Volga Colonies.

Brief essay on the historical development of the Volga colonies and biographical notes on about thirty prominent Volga Germans.

162.   Skal'kovskii, Apollon Aleksandrovich. *Khronologicheskoe obozrenie istorii novorossiiskago kraia, 1730–1823*. 2 vols. Odessa: Gorodskaia tipografiia, 1836, 1838.

CtY

A Chronological Review of the History of the New Russia Territory, 1730–1823.

A first-hand history of New Russia by a man who traveled it extensively. Volume 2 relates foundation of German colonies in 1804 in New Russia. Laden with statistics.

163.   Skal'kovskii, Apollon Aleksandrovich. *Opyt statisticheskago opisaniia novorossiiskago kraia*. 2 vols. Odessa: Tipografiia L. N. Nitche, 1850, 1853.

DLC

An attempt at a Statistical Description of the New Russia Region.

Best work for the area and period. Emphasis on the geography, ethnography, history, and agriculture of New Russia.

164.   Skal'kovskii, Apollon Aleksandrovich. *Vzgliad na skotovodstvo novorossiiskago kraia. 1846–1848.* St. Petersburg, 1850.

LL

A Look at Cattle Raising in the Territory of New Russia, 1846–1848.

Report on the status of cattle raising in New Russia with reference to important role of colonists, especially Mennonites, in improving herds.

165.   *Statisticheskie tablitsy samarskoi gubernii.* 5 vols. Samara: Izdanie samarskogo gubernskogo statisticheskogo komiteta, 1870–1871.

LL

Sec. 1, no. 1—Sostav narodonaseleniia samarskoi gubernii po plemenam, 1870.
Sec. 1, no. 2—Sostav narodonaseleniia samarskoi gubernii po veroispovedaniiam, 1870.
Sec. 1, no. 4—Sostav narodonaseleniia samarskoi gubernii po vosrastu, 1871.
Sec. 1, no. 5—Sostav narodonaseleniia samarskoi gubernii po semeinomu sostavu i rabochim silam, 1871.
Sec. 2, no. 4—Skotovodstvo, 1870. Statistical Tables of Samara Province.

Sec. 1, no. 1—Composition of the Population of Samara Province by Nationality, 1870.
Sec. 1, no. 2—Composition of the Population of Samara Province by Religious Affiliation, 1870.
Sec. 1, no. 4—Composition of the Population of Samara Province by Age, 1871.
Sec. 1, no. 5—Composition of the Population of Samara Province by Family Status and Work Force, 1871.
Sec. 2, no. 4—Livestock Raising, 1870.

These publications of the Samara Provincial Statistical Committee are based on data gathered in 1870. They give information by colony about the Volga German settlers living in Samara Province.

166.   *Statisticheskii spravochnik po narodnomu obrazovaniiu 1923.* 1st ed. Pokrovsk: Izdatel'stvo statbiuro obl. nemtsev povolzh'ia, 1923.

LL

Statistical Reference Book on Popular Education for 1923.

Examines public education in the Volga German areas after the establishment of Soviet power.

167.   Svavitskaia, Z. M. *Zemskie podvornye perepisi 1880–1913, pouezdnye itogi*. Moscow: Tsentral'noe statisticheskoe upravlenie, 1926.

LL

Zemstvo Household Census from 1880–1913: Results by District.

Results of *zemstvo* enumeration of households by district for the provinces of European Russia undertaken during the period indicated.

168.   Tikhmenev, A. G., ed. *Sochineniia E. I. Gubera*. 3 vols. St. Petersburg: Izdanie A. Smirdina Syna, 1859–1860.

NN

The Works of E. I. Huber.

The writings of E. I. Huber, a highly regarded poet and contemporary of Pushkin, who was born in a Volga German colony but abandoned the Volga for a career as a poet. He died very young.

169.   *Trudy khersonskogo gubernskogo statisticheskogo komiteta. Kniga 1. Chast' 1. (Materialy dlia geografii i statistiki khersonskoi gubernii)*. Kherson: Khersonskaia gubernskaia tipografiia, 1863.

LL

Works of the Kherson Province Statistical Committee. Book 1. Part 1. Materials for the Geography and Statistics of Kherson Province.

170.   Velitsyn, A. A., pseud. [Paltov, A. A.]. *Nemetskoe zavoevanie na iuge rossii*. St. Petersburg: Tipografiia tovarishchestva "Obshchestvennaia Pol'za," 1890.

DLC NN

The German Conquest in Southern Russia.

An anti-German view based on two months' observations (1899) of some 250 German colonies on the Dnieper and Volga. Originally published in *Russkii vestnik*. See entry 381.

171.   Velitsyn, A. A., pseud. [Paltov, A. A.]. *Nemtsy v rossii; ocherki istoricheskago razvitiia i nastoiashchago polozheniia nemetskikh kolonii na iuge i vostoke rossii*. St. Petersburg: Izdanie russkago vestnika, 1893.

DLC NN

The Germans in Russia: Essays on the Historical Development and Present Condition of the German Colonies in the South and East of Russia.

Anti-German study originally serialized in *Russkii vestnik*. See entries 379, 380, 382.

172.   Yevreinov, Grigorii A. *Rossiiskie nemtsy*. Petrograd: Tip. Glavnago upravleniia udelov, 1915.

NN

The Russian Germans.

Anti-German work occasioned by the spy mania of World War I.

173.   Zyuryukin, V. *Mennonity keppental'skogo raiona oblasti nemtsev povolzh'ia v bytovom i khoziaistvennom otnoshenii; issledovaniia i materialy*. Pokrovsk: Izd. zhurnala Unsere virtshaft, 1923.

NN

The Mennonites of Keppen'tal District, the Region of Volga Germans, and Its Life and Economic Relations: Studies and Materials.

Specialized study of a little known group.

Articles and Statutes

III. Articles and Statutes

174.   Al'man, B. D. "Vliianie trakhomy na ekonomicheskoe polozhenie poselian' nemetskikh kolonii." *Vestnik novouzenskago zemstva*, no. 3 (May–June 1912): 70–80.

LL

The Influence of Trachoma on the Economic Position of the Settled German Colonies.

Report of a *zemstvo* doctor on the extent and treatment of trachoma among the Volga Germans.

175.   Antropovich. "Ob emigratsii nashikh kolonistov v ameriku." *Saratovskii spravochnyi listok,* no. 57 (1877).

LL

The Emigration of Our Colonists to America.

176.   Artamonov, Mikhail. "Pis'ma s vol'gi (ot nashego spetsial'nogo korrespondenta)." *Izvestiia TsIK SSSR*, no. 205 (9 September 1924): 2.

CU CtY DLC NN NNC

Letters from the Volga (from our Special Correspondent).

Four short articles on economic and political conditions in the autonomous Volga German republic.

177.   B., Sh. "Sem'ia nemtsev-kolonistov." *Istoricheskii vestnik*, no. 7 (July 1906): 200–204.

DLC NN

A Family of German Colonists.

Brief essay on life in a German family.

178.   Basikhin, P. "Nemetskaia koloniia na kavkaze." *Kavkazskii vestnik* 1, no. 2 (1900): 14.

NN

A German Colony in the Caucasus.

179.   B–skii, A. "Emigratsiia privolzhskikh kolonistov-nemtsev v ame-riku." *Saratovskii listok,* no. 18(1888).

LL

The Emigration of the Volga German Colonists to America.

180.   "Bunt nemetskikh kolonistov (koloniia egkeim, novouzenskogo uezda, samarskoi gubernii)." *Golos moskvy*, 12 April 1915, p. 2.

LL

Riot of German Colonists (the Colony of Eckheim, Novouzensk District, Samara Province).

181.   Dinges, G. "K izucheniiu govorov povolzhskikh nemtsev." *Uchenye zapiski saratovskogo gosudarstvennogo universiteta imeni N. G. Chernyshevskogo* 4, no. 3 (1925): 12–20.

LL

Towards a Study of the Dialects of the Volga Germans.

Very scholarly article on the Volga German dialects by an authority on the subject.

182.   Ditts, Iakov Tim. "Iz istorii nemetskikh kolonii. Napadenie i bor'ba s kochevnikami." *Saratovskii listok*, nos. 139–40 (1914).

LL

From the History of the German Colonies. Attacks and Struggle with the Nomads.

Short articles on the difficult early years of the Volga colonies.

183.   Ditts, Iakov Tim. "Iz proshlogo nemetskikh kolonii saratovskoi i samarskoi gubernii." *Saratovskii dnevnik*, nos. 47, 48 (1888).

LL

From the Past of the German Colonies in Saratov and Samara Provinces.

184.   Ditts, Iakov Tim. "K 150-letnemu iubileiu nemetskikh kolonii (1764–1914)." *Saratovskii listok,* no. 140 (1914): 2.

LL

For the 150th Anniversary of the German Colonies (1764–1914).

Highlights from the history of the Volga settlements.

185. Ditts, Iakov Tim. "Pervaia nemetskaia koloniia v povolzh'e." *Saratovskii listok*, no. 58 (1914): 2–3.

LL

The First German Colony Along the Volga.

Deals with the Dobrinka colony.

186. Ditts, Iakov Tim. "Pugachev v nemetskikh koloniiakh." *Saratovskii listok*, nos. 137, 138 (1914).

LL

Pugachev in the German Colonies.

187. Ditts, Iakov Tim. "Selo rovnoe, ego nravy i obshchestvennoe upravlenie." *Saratovskii dnevnik*, nos. 10–11 (1888).

LL

The Settlement of Rovnoe: Its Customs and Public Administration.

Rovnoe was the Russian name for the Volga settlement of Seelmann.

188. "Dnevnik Pastora Gubera s 6-go po 31-e avgusta 1830 g." *Russkaia starina*, no. 8 (1878): 581–90.

DLC NN

The Diary of Pastor Huber from 6–31 August 1830.

This pastor served in the Volga colonies and his diary reflects life among the colonists.

189. "Doklad tov. Rykova na mitinge v respublike nemtsev povolzh'ia (30-go avgusta 1924 g.)." *Izvestiia TsIK SSSR*, no. 205 (9 September 1924): 2.

CU CtY DLC NN NNC

Report of Comrade Rykov on the Meeting in the Volga German Republic on 30 August 1924.

Rykov report occasioned by his trip to the Volga German region to promise government assistance in the recovery of agriculture, which had been plagued by a series of bad crops and famine in the early 1920s.

190.　Dukhovnikov, Flegont V. "Nemtsy, drugie inostrantsy i prishlye liudi v saratove." *Saratovskii krai. Istoricheskie ocherki, vospominaniia, materialy*, no. 1 (1893): 237–64.

LL

The Germans, Other Foreigners and Newly Arrived Peoples in Saratov.

History of German settlement in the city of Saratov.

191.　Dukhovskii. "Kolonii na volge." *Kazanskii vestnik* 25, pt. 1 (1829): 56–64.

LL

Colonies on the Volga.

Reviews history of the original colonies founded along the Volga.

192.　Dunin, A. A. "Nemtsy v samarskikh stepiakh." *Istoricheskii vestnik* 142 (November 1915): 543–58.

DLC NN

The Germans in the Samara Steppe.

Anti-German article.

193.　Dunin, A. A. "V nemetskikh kogtiakh. Povest'. (Iz staro-moskovskago nemetskago zasil'ia)." *Istoricheskii vestnik* 149–50 (January 1917): 1–35.

CSt-H DLC NN

In the Claws of the Germans: A Tale (From the Old Muscovite German Dominance).

Anti-German story about a wealthy, intriguing German colonist named Hoffman.

194.　"Dvizhenie narodonaseleniia v saratovskoi gubernii (1844–1853)." *Saratovskiia gubernskiia vedomosti*, no. 47 (1854): 218–20.

LL

Movement of Population in Saratov Province (1844–1853).

Discusses founding of some of the Volga daughter colonies.

195.　Fadeev, Andrei M. "Vospominaniia Andreia Mikhailovicha Fadeeva." *Russkii arkhiv*, no. 4 (1891): 465–94; no. 5 (1891): 14–60.

DLC

The Memoirs of Andrei Mikhailovich Fadeev.

Memoirs of a government bureaucrat and former governor of Saratov Province in the 1840s.

196. Faidel', A. "Kak zaselialis' nemetskie kolonii. Iz vospominanii kolonista. " *Saratovskii listok*, no. 151 (1914).

LL

How the German Colonies Were Settled: From the Reminiscences of a Colonist.

Reminiscences of a Volga settler.

197. Gekker, G. "Vosem' let respubliki nemtsev povolzh'ia." *Pravda*, no. 242 (20 October 1926): 4.

CSt-H DLC NN NNC

Eight Years of the Volga German Republic.

Brief article on the cultural accomplishments and agrarian setbacks of the autonomous Volga German republic.

198. "Geograficheskoe i statisticheskoe izvestie o saratovskoi gubernii." *Russkii invalid*, no. 15 (1827): 58–60.

LL

Geographical and Statistical Information about Saratov Province.

Includes statistical information on Volga colonies. See also entry 391 "Zamechaniia na stat'iu statisticheskuiu pomeshchennuiu v No. 15 *Russkii invalid.*"

199. Geraklitov, A. A. "Arkhivy saratovskoi gubernii." *Trudy saratov-skoi uchenoi arkhivnoi komissii*, no. 30 (1913): 3–31.

NN

The Archives of Saratov Province.

Mentions *volost* archives of Volga colonies.

200. Geraklitov, A. A. "Obzor pugachevskikh del iz astrakhanskago gubernskago arkhiva." *Trudy saratovskoi uchenoi arkhivnoi komissii*, no. 30 (1913): 33–51.

NN

A Survey of the Pugachev Affair from the Astrakhan Provincial Archive.

Brief mention of Volga colonists and Pugachev on pages 40–41.

201.   Goniasinskii. "Selo iagodnaia poliana, saratovskago uezda. " *Saratovskiia gubernskiia vedomosti*, no. 31 (1894).

LL

The Settlement of Iagodnaia Poliana in Saratov District.

202.   Gorodetskii, M. "K istorii rimskago katolitsizma v rossii (tiraspol'skaia ili saratovskaia latinskaia eparkhiia)." *Istoricheskii vestnik* (October 1889): 122–34.

DLC NN

Concerning the History of Roman Catholicism in Russia (the Tiraspol or Saratov Latin Diocese).

Discusses the Rome-St. Petersburg agreement in 1847 which created the seventh bishopric in Russia first headquartered in Tiraspol (Kherson Province) and later in the city of Saratov.

203.   I., A. "O zaselenii kryma novymi poselentsami." *Russkii vestnik* 63, no. 5 (1866): 256–68.

DLC NN

The Settlement of the Crimea by New Settlers.

Relates settlement of foreigners in Crimea after its annexation by Catherine II.

204.   I., B. "Novyi oblastnoi tsentr. (Iz besed s predispolkomom nemkommuny tov. Moor)." *Saratovskiia izvestiia*, no. 175 (1922).

LL

The New Provincial Center. (Conversations with the Chairman of the Executive Committee of the German Commune, Comrade Moore).

205.   Isaev, A. "Zametki o nemetskikh koloniiakh v rossii." *Russkaia mysl'*, no. 12 (December 1894): 87–112.

CSt-H DLC NN

Comments about the German Colonies in Russia.

Critical of foreign colonies.

206. Iudin, P. L. "Nemetskoe zaselenie. Povolzhskie kolonisty." *Russkii arkhiv* 4 (1915): 474–94.

CSt-H DLC NN

German Settlement: The Volga Colonies.

Scholarly work on the 1760s founding of the Volga colonies.

207. Ivanenko, G. "Po povodu zakona 13 dekabria 1915 g." *Zhurnal ministerstva iustitsii* 4 (1916): 209–19.

NN

Apropos the Law of 13 December 1915.

A juristic analysis of the war-time law expropriating the former colonists' homesteads.

208. "Iz ekaterinoslavlia, ot 5 ianvaria." *Severnaia pchela*, no. 23 (1810).

LL

From Ekaterinoslavl, 5 January.

This article discusses new Mennonite settlements in southern Russia.

209. "Iz kamyshinskogo uezda. O nemetskikh koloniiakh." *Saratovskii dnevnik*, no. 108 (1888): 2.

LL

From Kamyshin District: About the German Colonies.

Reports on economic situation in the colonies.

210. "Iz sarepty." *Vostochnye izvestiia*, no. 10 (1814): 90–93.

LL

From Sarepta.

Stresses the economic acumen of the Moravian Brethren settled in the colony of Sarepta.

211. "Iz sarepty (o budushchnosti ee)." *Saratovskii listok*, no. 158 (1891).

LL

From Sarepta (Concerning Its Future).

212. "K iubileiu nemetskikh kolonii." *Saratovskii vestnik*, no. 140 (1914).

LL

For the Anniversary of the German Colonies.

About the founding of the Volga colonies.

213.　"K pereimenovaniiu nemetskikh nazvanii gorodov v rossii." *Novoe vremia*, no. 14272 (2/15 December 1915): 3.

CSt-H

The Renaming of German-Name Cities in Russia.

Government insistence that only Russian names of the German colonies be used.

214.　"K voprosu o likvidatsii nemetskago zemlevladeniia." *Novoe vremia*, no. 14272 (2/15 December 1915): 3.

CSt-H

Concerning the Question of Liquidation of German Landholding.

War-time legislation confiscating landholdings of the German settlers.

215.　Kabuzan, V. M. "Materialy revizii kak istochnik po istorii naseleniia rossii XVIII–pervoi poloviny XIX veka (1719–1858 gg.)." Unpublished doctoral dissertation, Institut istorii, Akademiia nauk SSSR, 1959.

LL

Revision Materials as a Source for the History of the Population of Russia in the Eighteenth and First Half of the Nineteenth Century (1719–1858).

Excellent study of revisions as source materials.

216.　Kadykov, St. "Selo ekaterininskoe, samarskoi gubernii." *Samarskiia gubernskiia vedomosti*, no. 41 (1852): 693–95; no. 42 (1852): 710–12.

LL

The Settlement of Ekaterinin in Samara Province.

Early history of the colony of Katharinenstadt (Baronsk).

217.　"Kamyshin. Kharakter nemtsev." *Saratovskii dnevnik*, nos. 23, 117 (1882).

LL

Kamyshin: The Character of the Germans.

Russian view of the west-bank Volga Germans.

218. Kantor, R. "Bismark i 'bunt' nemetskikh kolonistov v rossii." *Russkoe proshloe*, no. 2 (1923): 154–58.

CSt-H NN

Bismarck and the "Riot" of German Colonists in Russia.

Bismarck's intervention in 1880 on behalf of German settlers in Volynia Province who faced loss of their leaseholdings.

219. Karkling, A. "O melkom kredite u nemetskago naseleniia." *Sbornik sel'sko-khoziaistvennykh svedenii*, no. 4 (1911): 205–18.

LL

Petty Credit among the German Population.

Discusses credit institutions and savings associations in the Volga colonies.

220. Kedrov, S. "Kratkii obzor istorii saratovskago kraia." *Saratovskii krai. Istoricheskie ocherki, vospominaniia, materialy*, no. 1 (1893): 3–18.

LL

A Short Review of the History of the Saratov Region.

221. Kenis, K. "V koloniiakh mennonitov (orenburgskaia guberniia)." *Pravda*, no. 198 (29 August 1926): 4.

CSt-H DLC NN NNC

In the Mennonite Colonies of Orenburg Province.

222. Keppen, Petr. [Köppen]. "O uchilishchakh, sostoiashchikh v vedenii glavnago upravleniia dukhovnykh del inostrannykh ispovedanii. (Materialy dlia istorii prosveshcheniia v rossii)." *Bibliograficheskii listy P. Keppena* 3 (1825): 22–38.

LL

Concerning Schools under the Administration of the Main Department of Spiritual Affairs of Foreign Faiths. (Materials for the History of Education in Russia).

This article contains statistical information on the church schools of the Evangelical colonies in Saratov Province.

223. "Khersonskie mennonitskie kolonii i tabuny stepnykh i dikikh loshadei v ukraine." *Severnaia pchela*, nos. 51, 53, 54 (1852).

LL

The Kherson Mennonite Colonies and Herds of Steppe and Wild Horses in the Ukraine.

224. Khovanskii, N. F. "K istorii nemetskikh kolonii saratovskoi gubernii (iz del senatskago arkhiva)." *Trudy saratovskoi uchenoi arkhivnoi komissii*, no. 31 (1914): 51–58.

LL

Concerning the History of the German Colonies of Saratov Province (from the Records of the Senate Archive).

Well-researched article based on archive materials.

225. Kirsanov, D. I. "Besedy po sel'skomu khoziaistvu." *Vestnik novouzenskago zemstva*, no. 2 (March–April 1913): 7–19; no. 3 (May–June 1913): 32–50; no. 5–6 (September–December 1913): 7–19.

LL

Conversations on Agriculture.

Comments from Volga German settlers on the development and present state of agriculture in Novouzensk District, Samara Province.

226. Klaus, A. A. "Dukhovenstvo i shkoly v nashikh nemetskikh koloniiakh." *Vestnik evropy* 3, no. 1 (1869): 138–74; no. 5 (1869): 235–74.

CSt-H

The Clergy and Schools in Our German Colonies.

Regards the clergy as a backward force in the German colonies. Later republished by Klaus in his book *Nashi kolonii* as Chapter 9. See entry 68.

227. Klaus, A. A. "Obshchina-sobstvennik i eia iuridicheskaia organizatsiia." *Vestnik evropy*, no. 2 (February 1870): 573–628; no. 3 (March 1870): 72–118.

CSt-H

The Commune-Proprietor and Its Legal Organization.

Examines the landholding and property rights of German colonists, especially the Black Sea Germans.

228. Klaus, A. A. "Sektatory-kolonisty v rossii." *Vestnik evropy* 1, no. 1 (1868): 256–300; 2, no. 3 (1868): 277–326; 3, no..6 (1868): 665–722; 1, no. 7 (1868): 713–66.

CSt-H

Sects-Colonists in Russia.

Religious sects among the German colonists. These articles all appeared in Klaus's *Nashi kolonii* as Chapters 2, 3, and 4. See entry 68.

229. Kleiman, V. "Avtonomnaia oblast' nemtsev povolzh'ia." *Zhizn' natsional'nostei* 1 (January 1923): 62–67.

DLC NN

The Autonomous Region of the Volga Germans.

230. Kolesnikov, G. I. "Novouzenskii uezd (v ego proshlom i nas-toiashchem)." *Vestnik novouzenskago zemstva*, no. 1 (January–February 1912): 26–64; no. 2 (March–April 1912): 23–50.

LL

Novouzensk District (in Its Past and Present).

Very good article which contains size of land allotments given to each settlement in Novouzensk District at its founding.

231. "Kolonii na volge." *Russkii invalid*, no. 151 (1830): 602–03; no. 153 (1830): 610–11.

LL

Colonies on the Volga.

232. "Koloniia gofnungstal'." Translated by Pavel Shkuratov. *Kher-sonskiia gubernskiia vedomosti*, no. 15 (1852): 115–17.

LL

The Colony of Hoffnungsthal.

Hoffnungsthal was a colony in the Odessa area of southern Russia.

233. "Koloniia sosnovka, kamyshinskogo u. (o pereseleniiakh)." *Sara-tovskii dnevnik*, no. 186 (1888): 2.

LL

The Sosnovka Colony, Kamyshin District (Its Migrations).

The German name of this colony was Schilling.

234. Komarnitsky, Andrei. "O raznitse v urozhaiakh khleba pri nemetskom i malorossiiskom sposobakh obrabotki zemli." *Zapiski imperatorskago obshchestva sel'skago khoziaistva iuzhnoi rossii*, no. 7 (July 1870): 504–06.

LL

Concerning the Difference in Grain Harvests between the German and Little Russian Method of Cultivation of the Soil.

Focus is on Mennonite grain farming.

235. Koval'nitskii, A. "Svadebnye obriady na volyni nemtsev, prinadlezhashchikh k sekte baptistov." *Kievlianin*, no. 139 (1866).

LL

Wedding Rites of Volynia Germans Belonging to the Baptist Sect.

236. Krasnoperov, I. "Mennonitskiia koloniia (statistiko-ekonomicheskoe opisanie)." *Iuridicheskii vestnik*, no. 6–7 (June–July 1889): 294–311.

DLC NN

The Mennonite Colonies (A Statistical-Economic Description).

237. Krasnoperov, I. "Mennonitskoe khoziaistvo v samarskom uezde." *Russkaia mysl'*, no. 10 (October 1883): 53–68.

DLC NN

The Mennonite Economy in Samara District.

238. "Kratkii obzor sostoianiia menonistskikh kolonii na r. molochoi [*sic*] v 1847 g. v sel'sko-khoziaistvennom otnoshenii," *Zapiski obshchestva sel'skago khoziaistva iuzhnago rossii* 4 (1847): 66–69.

LL

A Brief Survey of the Agricultural Conditions of the Mennonite Colonies on the Molochnaia River in 1847.

239. "Kratkoe opisanie selenii ilavlinskoi vol., kamyshinsk. u." *Saratovskiia gubernskiia vedomosti*, no. 46 (1890): 356–58.

LL

A Brief Description of Settlements in Ilavlin Volost, Kamyshin District.

This article briefly describes the west-bank Volga settlements of Marienfeld, Josephstal, Erlenbach, Oberdorf, Neu-Norka, and Alexandertal.

240. Kryshtofovich, F. "Kak ekhat' v ameriku na zarabotki." *Sel'skii khoziain*, no. 17 (1913): 823–25; no. 18 (1913): 899–901.

LL

How to Go to America in Search of a Living.

Paints a bleak picture of what awaits Russian citizens emigrating to the Americas.

241. Leopol'dov, A. "Chislo zhitelei saratovskoi gubernii v 1846 g." *Saratovskiia gubernskiia vedomosti*, no. 18 (1847): 67–68.

LL

The Number of Inhabitants of Saratov Province in 1846.

Includes statistics on the Volga Germans.

242. Leopol'dov, A. "Kratkoe statisticheskoe obozrenie saratovskoi gubernii." *Vestnik evropy* 149, no. 14 (1826): 99–123.

LL

A Brief Statistical Summary of Saratov Province.

243. Leopol'dov, A. "Opisanie kolonial'nykh inostrannykh poselenii v samarskoi gubernii." *Samarskiia gubernskiia vedomosti*, no. 10 (1853): 55–56; no. 11 (1853): 59–61.

LL

Description of Foreign Colony Settlements in Samara Province.

Impressionistic account of the east-bank Volga German settlements.

244. Leopol'dov, A. "Statisticheskaia zapiska o narodakh, naseliaiushchikh saratovskoi gubernii." *Moskovskii telegraf* 52, no. 13 (1833): 135–43.

LL

Statistical Notes about the Peoples Populating Saratov province.

Author relates statistics and impressions of the Germans he met.

245. Leopol'dov, A. "Vzgliad na novouzenskii okrug saratovskoi gubernii." *Saratovskiia gubernskiia vedomosti*, no. 8 (1845): 83–86; no. 9 (1845): 90–93.

LL

A Look at Novouzensk District in Saratov Province.

See same article in entry 246.

246. Leopol'dov, A. "Vzgliad na novouzenskii okrug saratovskoi gubernii." *Zhurnal ministerstva gosudarstvennykh imushchestv*, chast' 13 (1844): 29–36.

LL

A Look at Novouzensk District in Saratov province.

Description of the geography and economy of the area. See same article in entry 245.

247. Leopol'dov, A. "Vzgliad na zavolzhskii krai v saratovskoi gubernii." *Severnaia pchela*, nos. 289, 291(1835).

LL

A Look at the Trans-Volga Region in Saratov Province.

248. Leopol'dov, A. F. "Putevyia zametki ot saratova do samary." *Samarskiia gubernskiia vedomosti*, nos. 26, 27, 28, 29 (1852).

LL

Travel Notes from Saratov to Samara.

Author includes observations of some German colonies he visited.

249. Lerner, I. M. "Nemetskiia koloniia v novorossiiskom krae (po dannym iz arkhiva byvshago novorossiiskago general'-gubernator)." *Vedomosti odesskago gradonachal'stva*, no. 231 (25 October 1903): 2–3; no. 236 (31 October 1903): 3; no. 257 (28 November 1903): 2; no. 268 (12 December 1903): 2.

LL

German Colonies in New Russia Territory (According to Information from the Archive of the Former Governor-General of New Russia).

A very good article on the 1804 founding of colonies in New Russia.

250. Lerner, Iosif M. "Germanskie vykhodtsy v novorossii. (Po dannym iz arkhiva byvshago novorossiiskago general gubernatorskago upravleniia)." *Russkii arkhiv*, no. 3 (March 1908): 33–48.

CSt-H DLC NN

People of German Extraction in New Russia. (Based on Information in the Archives of the Administration of the Former Governor-General of New Russia).

Article deals with Germans who settled in New Russia in 1804.

251. Liaskovskii, B. "Materialy dlia statisticheskago opisaniia saratov-skoi gubernii." *Zhurnal ministerstva vnutrennikh del* 7, no. 3(1860).
LL

Materials for a Statistical Description of Saratov Province.

Includes statistical data on the Volga Germans.

252. Liubomirov, P. "Nizhnee povolzh'e poltorasta let nazad." *Nizhnee povolzh'e*, no. 1 (May 1924): 21–31.
LL

The Lower Volga 150 Years Ago.

Gives physical description of the Lower Volga and discusses problem of getting reliable population figures on the eighteenth-century Volga colonists.

253. M. "Nemtsy na povolzh'e. Pis'mo iz saratova." *Russkii mir*, nos. 292, 293, 296 (1872).
LL

Germans along the Volga: Letter from Saratov.

254. Markevich, A. I. "Iz proshlogo krymskogo vinogradarstva i vino-deliia. Po arkhivnym materialam." *Vestnik vinodeliia ukrainy*, no. 9 (1927): 548–54; no. 10 (1927): 583–98; no. 11 (1927): 664–68; no. 12 (1927): 725–29.
LL

From the Past of the Crimean Viticulture and Wine-Making: Based on Archival Materials.

This article mentions colonies established in the Crimea.

255. Markovsky, A. "Krest'ianskoe khoziaistvo iuzhnoi rossii i mery k ego uluchsheniiu." *Sel'skoe khoziaistvo i lesovodstvo* 198 (1900): 1–22.
LL

Peasant Agriculture in Southern Russia and Measures to Improve It.

Mentions Black Sea German and Mennonite agricultural methods.

256. "Materialy dlia statistiki saratovskoi gubernii." *Statisticheskii zhurnal* 1, pt. 1 (1806): 94–157.
LL

Statistical Materials for Saratov Province.

Population figures for Saratov Province.

257.   Mavrodin, V. V. "Krest'ianskaia voina v rossii v 1773–1775
godakh." *Voprosy istorii*, no. 9(September 1973): 64–77.
                                          Available in various libraries
The Peasant War in Russia in 1773–1775.

Asserts that a sizable segment of Volga Germans participated in the
Pugachev rebellion.

258.   Mavrodin, V. V. "Ob uchastii kolonistov povolzh'ia v vosstanii
Pugacheva." in *Krest'ianstvo i klassovaia bor'ba v feodal'noi rossii*. Edited by
N. E. Nosov. Leningrad: Izdatel'stvo "Nauka," 1967, pp. 400–13.
                                                                  DLC
About the Participation of the Volga German Colonists in the Pugachev
Revolt.

Depicts Volga Germans as active revolutionaries in the Pugachev revolt.

259.   "Mennonity-kolonisty v novoros. krae." *Novorossiiskii telegraf*, no.
1372 (1879).
                                                                  LL
Mennonite Colonists in New Russia.

260.   "Mestnaia khronika." *Vestnik novouzenskago zemstva*, no. 1–2
(January–April 1915): 130–201.
                                                                  LL
Local Chronicle.

Reflects growing anti-German feeling towards the Volga Germans.

261.   Mikhailov, N. "Koloniia sarepty po vliianiiu na blizhaishiia mesta
astrakhanskoi i saratovskoi gub." *Astrakhanskiia gubernskiia vedomosti*, no.
40 (1846): 267–68.
                                                                  LL
The Sarepta Colony and Its Influence on Neighboring Places in Astrakhan and Saratov Provinces.

262.   Minkh, A. N. "Iagodno-polianskaia volost'. (Nemtsy-kolonisty). Istor. statistich. ocherk." *Saratovskiia gubernskiia vedomosti*, nos. 152, 153 (1879).

LL

Iagodno-Poliana Volost. (The German Colonists): Historical Statistical Essay.

This article was published separately as a 64-page pamphlet in 1879.

263.   Minkh, A. N. "Shcherbakovka nemetskaia." *Saratovskiia gubernskiia vedomosti*, no. 16 (1895).

LL

German Shcherbakovka.

Article on the west-bank Volga colony of Deutsch-Shcherbakovka.

264.   Molchanov, A. "Putevyia zametki. Oazis sytago dovol'stva." *Novoe vremia*, nos. 1264, 1265 (1879).

LL

Travel Notes: Oasis of Contentment.

An article giving observations on the Evangelical brotherhood community at Sarepta.

265.   "Molochanskii kolonistskii okrug." *Severnyi arkhiv* 9 (1824): 201–14.

LL

The Molochansk Colonist District.

An account of life among the Black Sea German colonies in Molochansk District.

266.   Mordovtsev, D. "Resul'taty poslednei revizii po saratovskoi gubernii." *Saratovskiia gubernskiia vedomosti*, nos. 2, 3, 4 (1859).

LL

Results of the Last Revision in Saratov Province.

General results of the 1857–1858 census for Saratov Province.

267.   Murav'ev, N. "Sarepta. Kratkii ocherk kolonii i ee zhizni i promyshlennosti." *Vostok*, nos. 14–15 (1866).

LL

Sarepta: A Brief Sketch of the Colony and Its Life and Industry.

268. "Nechto o privolzhskikh poselianakh nemtsakh." *Saratovskii listok,* no. 245 (1887).

LL

Something about the Settlements of the Volga Germans.

269. Neelov, N. N. "Svedeniia o kolichestve poselivshikhsia v 1769 g. kolonistakh v saratovskoi gubernii." *Trudy saratovskoi uchenoi arkhivnoi komissii*, no. 1 (1889): 176–85.

LL

Information about the Number of Colonists Who Settled in Saratov Province in 1769.

This is a statistical report of the Chancellery for the Guardianship of Foreign Settlers dated 9 March 1769; it gives by colony the number of families, population, livestock holdings, crops planted, and homes constructed for the Volga colonies.

270. "Nemetskie kolonisty v rossii. Stat'ia P. V–ova." *Niva* 5 (1878).

NN

German Colonists in Russia.

Journal available in NN, but author was unable to verify this article.

271. "Nemetskiia kolonii nikolaevskogo uezda, samarsk. gub." *Saratovskiia gubernskiia vedomosti*, no. 27 (1890).

LL

The German Colonies of Nikolaev District, Samara Province.

Primarily a statistical review of economic conditions in the colonies of Nikolaev District.

272. "Nemetskoe selenie rozenberg, kamyshinskogo uezda." *Saratovskiia gubernskiia vedomosti*, no. 56 (1890): 436–37; no. 58 (1890): 451–52.

LL

The German Settlement of Rosenberg in Kamyshin District.

273. "Nemtsy-gosti." *Saratovskii dnevnik*, no. 167 (1889): 1.
LL
Germans-Guests.

Article stresses aloofness and separateness of the Volga colonies from their Slavic neighbors.

274. "Nemtsy-kolonisty na povolzh'e." *Russkii mir*, 263 (1873).
LL
German Colonists along the Volga.

275. "Nemtsy povolzh'ia." *Zhizn' natsional'nostei* 8 (August 1918).
LL
The Volga Germans.

276. "Neskol'ko faktov o pereselenii menonitov." *Odesskii vestnik*, no. 2 (1877).
LL
A Few Facts about the Emigration of the Mennonites.

Also published in *Russkii mir*, see entry 277.

277. "Neskol'ko faktov o pereselenii menonitov." *Russkii mir*, no. 10 (1877).
LL
A Few Facts about the Emigration of the Mennonites.

Also published in *Odesskii vestnik*, see entry 276.

278. "Neskol'ko slov o kolonistakh." *Volga*, no. 100 (1863).
LL
A Few Words about the Colonists.

279. "Neskol'ko slov o narodnosti nem. kolonistov saratovskoi g." *Saratovskiia gubernskiia vedomosti*, nos. 18, 19 (1858).
LL
A Few Words about the Nationality of the German Colonists in Saratov Province.

280. "Novouzenskie mennonity." *Saratovskii dnevnik*, no. 166 (1889): 1.
LL

The Mennonites of Novouzensk District.

281.   "Obozrenie inostrannykh kolonii v novorossiiskom krae. Ekaterinoslavskaia guberniia." *Severnyi arkhiv* 8 (1823): 33–45, 119–28, 200–
208.

LL

Review of Foreign Colonies in the Territory of New Russia: Ekaterinoslav Province.

Deals specifically with colonies in Khortitsa and Molochansk Districts,
the Crimea, and Krolevetsk District, Chernigov Province.

282.   "Obozrenie kolonii v iuzhnoi rossii i tavrich. gubernii." *Severnyi
arkhiv* 9 (1824): 142–51, 317–24; 10 (1824): 17–25, 64–84, 125–37.

LL

Review of Colonies in Southern Russia and Tauride Province.

283.   "Obozrenie sostoianiia poselennykh v saratovskoi gubernii inostrannykh kolonistov." *Severnaia pochta*, nos. 52, 56, 58, 60, 62 (1810).

NN

Review of the Conditions of the Foreign Colony Settlements in Saratov
Province.

Describes the difficult early years of the Volga Germans.

284.   "Obshchii ustav povolzhskago komissariata po delam natsional'-
nostei." *Izvestiia vserossiiskogo ts. komiteta sovetov krest'ianskikh, rabochikh,
soldatskikh i kazach'ikh deputatov*, no. 113 (5 June 1918): 4.

CSt-H DLC NN

General Statute of the Volga Commissariat of Nationality Affairs.

Decree establishing this agency.

285.   "Ocherk statistiki kamyshinsk. u." *Saratovskiia gubernskiia vedomosti*, no. 11 (1851): 48–51.

LL

Statistical Sketch of Kamyshin District.

Contains information on west-bank Volga colonies in Saratov Province, Kamyshin District.

286. "Ocherk zaseleniia samarskoi gubernii." *Samarskiia gubernskiia vedomosti*, nos. 16, 17 (1859).

LL

An Essay on the Settlement of Samara Province.

Includes information on east-bank Volga settlements.

287. "O kolonii elizabettam i rasvalinakh odnogo iz drevneishikh gruzinskikh monastyrei." *Zakavkazskii vestnik*, nos. 16–17, 123–33 (1847).

LL

About the Colony of Elizabeth and the Ruins of One of the Oldest Georgian Monasteries.

288. "O menonistskikh poseleniiakh v novouzenskom uezde." *Samarskiia gubernskiia vedomosti*, no. 42 (1859).

LL

The Mennonite Settlements in Novouzensk District.

289. Ommer. "Mennonitskie kolonii na molochnykh vodakh." Translated by L. A. *Odesskii vestnik*, no. 17 (1839): 199–201; no. 18 (1839): 211–15.

LL

The Mennonite Colonies on the Molochnyi Waterways.

290. "O nemetskikh shkolakh v kamyshinskom uezde." *Saratovskii dnevnik*, nos. 144, 153 (1888).

LL

About German Schools in Kamyshin District.

291. "O pereselenii menonitov v rossiiu, s 1787 g." *Russkaia starina* 1 (1879): 146–47.

NN

The Immigration of Mennonites to Russia, from 1787.

292. "O pereselentsakh saratovskoi gub." *Statisticheskii zhurnal*, 1, pt. 1 (1806): 247–52.

LL

The Settlers of Saratov Province.

Statistical information on all settlers living in Saratov Province.

293. "Opisanie kolonii inostrannykh poselentsev v samarskoi gub."
Samarskiia gubernskiia vedomosti, nos. 10–11 (1863).
                                                                    LL
A Description of the Foreign Colony Settlements in Samara Province.

294. "Opisanie kolonii, v saratovskii gubernii poselennykh." *Sanktpe-*
terburgskii zhurnal, no. 7 (1805): 102–29.
                                                                    LL
Description of Colonies Settled in Saratov Province.

295. Padalka, Lev. "Desiatinshchiki khersonskoi gubernii." *Kievskaia*
starina 50 (July–August–September 1895): 324–45.
                                                                   DLC
Dessiatiners of Kherson Province.

Mentions Black Sea German settlers in Kherson Province.

296. Pavlov, A. N. "Pochemu nashi nemtsy pereseliaiutsia v ameriku."
Saratovskii spravochnyi listok, no. 272 (1877): 2.
                                                                    LL
Why Our Germans Are Settling in America.

297. "Peterburgskii nemets." *Illiustratsiia* 5, no. 29 (1847): 67–71.
                                                                    LL
The Germans of St. Petersburg.

298. Pisarevskii, Grigorii G. "Inostrannye kolonisty greko-rossiiskago
ispovedaniia v povolzh'e." *Trudy saratovskoi uchenoi arkhivnoi komissii*, no.
33 (1916): 85–88.
                                                                    NN
Foreign Colonists of the Greek-Russian Faith in the Volga Area.

Tells about life and conditions of the small number of Volga Germans
who converted to Russian Orthodoxy.

299. Pisarevskii, Grigorii G. "Nizhnee povolzh'e v tret'ei chetverti
XVIII veka." *Izvestiia pedagogicheskogo fakul'teta. Obshchestvennye nauki* 14

(1929) [Azerbaidzhanskii gosudarstvennyi universitet imeni V. I. Lenina]: 221–29.

LL

The Lower Volga in the Third Quarter of the Eighteenth Century.

Describes conditions in the Lower Volga at the time of the first arrival of foreign settlers.

300. Pisarevskii, Grigorii G. "Vnutrennii rasporiadok v koloniiakh povolzh'ia pri Ekaterine II." *Varshavskiia universitetskiia izvestiia*, no. 7 (1913): 1–16; no. 8 (1914): 17–47; no. 9 (1915): 1–44.

NN

Internal Order in the Volga Colonies during the Reign of Catherine II.

See entry 104.

301. Pisarevskii, Grigorii G. "Vyzov mennonitov v rossii. (Po neizdannym arkhivnym dokumentam)." *Russkaia mysl'* 10 (October 1903): 49–72; 11 (November 1903): 85–102.

CSt-H DLC

The Invitation of the Mennonites to Russia. (Based on Unpublished Archive Documents).

302. Pisarevskii, Grigorii G. "Vyzov v rossiiu kolonistov iz dantsiga. Epizod iz istorii inostrannoi kolonizatsii v rossii." *Russkaia mysl'* 9 (September 1902): 71–94.

CSt-H DLC

The Invitation of the Danzig Colonists to Russia: An Episode from the History of Foreign Colonization in Russia.

303. "Pis'mo iz kolonii gal'bshtadt, ekaterinoslav. gub." *Molva*, no. 65 (1832): 257–59; no. 67 (1832): 265–67.

LL

Letter from the Colony of Halbstadt, Ekaterinoslav Province.

304. Pogodin, A. L. "Nemetskiia kolonii v rossii." *Moskovskii ezhenedelnik* 16 (1909): 18–22.

NN

German Colonies in Russia.

Anti-German view of foreign colonies.

305.   Rachinskii, I. "Khoziaistvennyi i nravstvennyi byt' kolonistov mariupol'skago okruga." *Ekonomicheskiia zapiski*, nos. 7, 18 (1859).

LL

Economic and Moral Life of the Colonists of Mariupol District.

306.   Rakitnikov, Al. "U nemetskikh kolonistov." *Krasnaia nov'*, no. 9 (November 1925): 243–49.

DLC NN

Among the German Colonists.

Visit by a Soviet journalist in 1925 to the colony of Elenendorf in southern Russia. Main point is that nothing much had changed in the colony since the 1917 revolutions.

307.   Rosenberg, L. "Nemetskaia koloniia semenovka, kubanskoi oblasti, kavkazskago otdela." *Sbornik materialov dlia opisaniia mestnostei i plemen kavkaza* 27, no. 2 (1900): 162–91.

NN

The German Colony of Semenovka in the Kuban Region of the Caucasus Department.

308.   Russia. Laws, statutes, etc. *Polnoe sobranie zakonov rossiiskoi imperii. Sobranie pervoe. S 1649–12 dek. 1825.* 44 vols. in 51. St. Petersburg, 1830, vol. 16, no. 11720.

CSt-H CtY CU DLC NN NNC

The Complete Collection of Laws of the Russian Empire. First Edition. From 1649 to 12 December 1825.

This is the 4 December 1762 manifesto of Catherine II, which first invited foreigners to settle in Russia.

309.   Russia. Laws, statutes, etc. *Polnoe sobranie zakonov rossiiskoi imperii. Sobranie pervoe. S 1649–12 dek. 1825*, vol. 16, no. 11880.

CSt-H CtY CU DLC NN NNC

The Complete Collection of Laws of the Russian Empire. First Edition. From 1649 to 12 December 1825.

This is the Catherine II manifesto of 22 July 1763, which enumerated all the privileges and obligations of foreigners wishing to settle in Russia.

310. Russia. Laws, statutes, etc. *Polnoe sobranie zakonov rossiiskoi imperii. Sobranie pervoe. S 1649–12 dek. 1825*, vol. 16, no. 11881.
CSt-H CtY CU DLC NN NNC
The Complete Collection of Laws of the Russian Empire. First Edition. From 1649 to 12 December 1825.

Act of 22 July 1763 establishing the duties of the Chancellery for the Guardianship of Foreign Settlers.

311. Russia. Laws, statutes, etc. *Polnoe sobranie zakonov rossiiskoi imperii. Sobranie pervoe. S 1649–12 dek. 1825,* vol. 16, no. 12095.
CSt-H CtY CU DLC NN NNC
The Complete Collection of Laws of the Russian Empire. First Edition. From 1649 to 12 December 1825.

This is the law of 19 March 1764 which established land law and allotments for the foreign colonists.

312. Russia. Laws, statutes, etc. *Polnoe sobranie zakonov rossiiskoi imperii. Sobranie pervoe. S 1649–12 dek. 1825*, vol. 24, no. 18022.
CSt-H CtY CU DLC NN NNC
The Complete Collection of Laws of the Russian Empire. First Edition. From 1649 to 12 December 1825.

Legislation of 30 June 1797 reestablishing the Saratov office of the Chancellery for the Guardianship of Foreign Settlers and instructions on its functions.

313. Russia. Laws, statutes, etc. *Polnoe sobranie zakonov rossiiskoi imperii. Sobranie pervoe. S 1649–12 dek. 1825*, vol. 28, no. 21163.
CSt-H CtY CU DLC NN NNC
The Complete Collection of Laws of the Russian Empire. First Edition. From 1649 to 12 December 1825.

This is the 20 February 1804 report of the Minister of Internal Affairs, often referred to as the 1804 manifesto. It amended and replaced the 22 July manifesto of Catherine II as the document which regulated foreign immigration to Russia.

314. Russia. Laws, statutes, etc. *Polnoe sobranie zakonov rossiiskoi imperii. Sobranie pervoe. S 1649–12 dek. 1825*, vol. 28, no. 27312.
CSt-H CtY CU DLC NN NNC

The Complete Collection of Laws of the Russian Empire. First Edition. From 1649 to 12 December 1825.

Act of 22 March 1818 establishing and defining the functions of the Committee of Guardianship, which was to administer the colonies in southern Russia.

315.   Russia. Laws, statutes, etc. *Polnoe sobranie zakonov rossiiskoi imperii. Sobranie pervoe. S 1649–12 dek. 1825*, vol. 28, no. 27912.
CSt-H CtY CU DLC NN NNC
The Complete Collection of Laws of the Russian Empire. First Edition. From 1649 to 12 December 1825.

Law of 5 August 1819, which prohibited further foreign settlement in the Russian empire.

316.   Russia. Laws, statutes, etc. *Polnoe sobranie zakonov rossiiskoi imperii. Sobranie vtoroe. S 12 dekabria 1825–1881.* 40 vols. in 125. St. Petersburg, 1830–1884, vol. 46, no. 49705.
CSt-H CtY CU DLC NN NNC
The Complete Collection of Laws of the Russian Empire. Second Edition. From 12 December 1825 to 1881.

Act of 4/16 June 1871 which eliminated special administrative arrangement of the colonies and subordinated them to the regular *volost*, district, and provincial administration.

317.   Russia. Ministerstvo gosudarstvennykh imushchestv. "Byt' molochanskikh menonistskikh kolonii," *Zhurnal ministerstva gosudarstvennykh imushchestv*, chast' 1, otdel 2 (1841): 553–63.
LL
Life in the Molochnaia River Mennonite Colonies.

318.   Russia. Ministerstvo gosudarstvennykh imushchestv. "Inostrantsy zemledel'tsy poselivshiesia na pomeshchich'ikh zemliakh." *Zhurnal ministerstva gosudarstvennkyh imushchestv*, chast' 73, otdel 4 (March 1860): 47–51.
LL
Foreign Agriculturalists Who Settled on the Lands of Landowners.

Pertains only to foreign settlers in New Russia.

319. Russia. Ministerstvo gosudarstvennykh imushchestv. "Istoriia i statistika kolonii inostrannykh poselentsev v rossii." *Zhurnal ministerstva gosudarstvennykh imushchestv*, chast' 52, otdel 2 (1854): 36–78; chast' 53, otdel 2 (1854): 1–34; chast' 54, otdel 1 (1855): 71–88; chast' 55, otdel 1 (1855): 57–88, 121–37.

LL

History and Statistics of the Colonies of Foreign Settlers in Russia.

Contains some of the best and most complete official statistics on the foreign colonies.

320. Russia. Ministerstvo gosudarstvennykh imushchestv. "Izgotovlenie i prodazha uluchshennykh zemledel'cheskikh orudii v nemetskikh koloniiakh, iuzhnago kraia rossii." *Zhurnal ministerstva gosudarstvennykh imushchestv*, chast' 43, otdel 4 (1852): 51–52.

LL

The Manufacture and Sale of Improved Agricultural Equipment in the German Colonies of the Southern Region of Russia.

321. Russia. Ministerstvo gosudarstvennykh imushchestv. "Khronologicheskaia vedomost' o pozhertvovaniiakh, sdelannykh gosudarstvennymi krest'ianami i kolonistami v pol'zu voisk." *Zhurnal ministerstva gosudarstvennykh imushchestv*, chast' 51, otdel 2 (1854): 9–14.

LL

A Chronological Review of the Donations Made by the State Peasants and Colonists on Behalf of the Troops.

Materiel and supplies given by the colonists in the Crimean War effort.

322. Russia. Ministerstvo gosudarstvennykh imushchestv. "Ob uspekhakh khoziaistva v koloniiakh iuzhnago kraia rossii." *Zhurnal ministerstva gosudarstvennykh imushchestv*, chast' 23, otdel 2 (1847): 252–62.

LL

Concerning the Economic Successes in the Colonies of the Southern Region of Russia.

323. Russia. Ministerstvo gosudarstvennykh imushchestv. "Ocherk sel'skago khoziaistva samarskikh inostrannykh poselentsev v 1855 g." *Zhurnal ministerstva gosudarstvennykh imushchestv*, chast' 61, otdel 1 (1856): 61–65.

LL

An Essay on the Agriculture of the Samara Foreign Settlers in 1855.

Presents description of state of colonists' agriculture in the 1850s.

324. Russia. Ministerstvo gosudarstvennykh imushchestv. "O kolonistskom rogatom skote." *Zhurnal ministerstva gosudarstvennykh imushchestv*, chast' 45, otdel 4 (1852): 78–79.

LL

About the Colonists' Horned Cattle.

Deals with cattle raising in the Black Sea German and Mennonite colonies.

325. Russia. Ministerstvo gosudarstvennykh imushchestv. "O menonistskikh poseleniiakh v novouzenskom uezde." *Zhurnal ministerstva gosudarstvennykh imushchestv*, chast' 12 (1859).

LL

The Mennonite Settlements in Novouzensk District.

Covers Mennonite colonies founded in the 1850s in Samara Province.

326. Russia. Ministerstvo gosudarstvennykh imushchestv. "O poselenii kolonistov v saratovskom krae." *Zhurnal ministerstva gosudarstvennykh imushchestv*, chast' 70, otdel 3 (February 1859): 31–40.

LL

Concerning the Settlement of the Colonists in Saratov Region.

327. Russia. Ministerstvo gosudarstvennykh imushchestv. "Opyty travoseianiia v koloniiakh iuzhnoi rossii v 1845 g." *Zhurnal ministerstva gosudarstvennykh imushchestv*, chast' 19, otdel 2 (1846): 137–41.

LL

Attempts at Fodder-Grass Cultivation in the Colonies of Southern Russia in 1845.

328. Russia. Ministerstvo gosudarstvennykh imushchestv. "O razvedenii tabaka v rybendorfskoi kolonii v ostrogozhskom uezde, voronezhskoi gubernii." *Zhurnal ministerstva gosudarstvennykh imushchestv*, chast' 17, otdel 4 (1845): 62–65.

LL

Concerning the Development of Tobacco in Rybendorf Colony in Ostrogozh District, Voronezh Province.

329. Russia. Ministerstvo gosudarstvennykh imushchestv. "O separatistakh nemetskikh kolonii v gruzii." *Zhurnal ministerstva gosudarstvennykh imushchestv*, chast' 12, otdel 4 (1844): 25–27.

LL

About the Separatist German Colonies in Georgia.

330. Russia. Ministerstvo gosudarstvennykh imushchestv. "O sodeist-vii, okazannom kolonistami i menonistami dvukh molochakikh [sic] ok-rugov novopereselivshimsia bolgaram." *Zhurnal ministerstva gosudarstven-nykh imushchestv*, chast' 79, otdel 1 (February 1862): 128–29.

LL

Concerning the Assistance Rendered by the Colonists and Mennonites to the Newly Settled Bulgars of Two Molochai Districts.

Intercolony assistance in the colonies of New Russia.

331. Russia. Ministerstvo gosudarstvennykh imushchestv. "Poriadok vodvoreniia inostrannykh i russkikh pereselentsev na svobodnykh kazen-nykh zemliakh novorossiiskogo kraia." *Zhurnal ministerstva gosudarstven-nykh imushchestv*, chast' 79, otdel 4 (February 1862): 12–15.

LL

The Method of Settling Foreign and Russian Settlers on the Free State Lands of the New Russia Territory.

Concerns settlement of New Russia in the early years of the nineteenth century.

332. Russia. Ministerstvo gosudarstvennykh imushchestv. "Sostoianie raznykh otraslei sel'skago khoziaistva v bolgarskikh i nemetskikh koloniiakh v bessarabii." *Zhurnal ministerstva gosudarstvennykh imushchestv*, chast 9, otdel 2 (1843): 125–27.

LL

The Conditions of Various Branches of Agriculture in the Bulgarian and German Colonies in Bessarabia.

333. Russia. Ministerstvo gosudarstvennykh imushchestv. "Statis-ticheskiia svedeniia o kolonistakh vedomstva saratovskoi kontory inos-trannykh poselentsev." *Zhurnal ministerstva gosudarstvennkyh imushchestv*, chast' 51, otdel 2 (1854): 1–8.

LL

Statistical Information about the Colonists of the Department of the Saratov Office of Foreign Settlers.

Excellent statistical source on the Volga Germans.

334.   Russia. Ministerstvo gosudarstvennykh imushchestv. "Statistika pereseleniia poselian vedomstva ministerstva gosudarstvennykh imushchestv." *Zhurnal ministerstva gosudarstvennykh imushchestv*, chast' 77, otdel 4 (1861): 44–45.

LL

Settlement Statistics of the Settlement Department of the Ministry of State Domains.

Includes statistics on foreign colonies.

335.   Russia. Ministerstvo gosudarstvennykh imushchestv. "Tabachnaia promyshlenost' [sic] i inostrannykh poselentsev samarskoi i saratovskoi gubernii." *Zhurnal ministerstva gosudarstvennykh imushchestv*, chast' 59, otdel 2 (1856): 27–40.

LL

The Tobacco Industry and the Foreign Settlers of Samara and Saratov Provinces.

336.   Russia. Ministerstvo gosudarstvennykh imushchestv. "Uspekhi travoseianiia v koloniiakh iuzhnoi rossii." *Zhurnal ministerstva gosudarstvennykh imushchestv*, chast' 17, otdel 4 (1845): 55–59.

LL

The Success of Fodder-Grass Cultivation in the Colonies of Southern Russia.

337.   Russia. Ministerstvo gosudarstvennykh imushchestv. "Vopros ob inostrannykh kolonistakh na pomeshchich'ikh zemliakh." *Zhurnal ministerstva gosudarstvennykh imushchestv*, chast' 74, otdel 4 (August 1860): 1–3.

LL

The Question of Foreign Colonists on Landowners' Lands.

Problems of leaseholding of New Russian colonists settled on lands of private landowners.

338.   Russia. Ministerstvo gosudarstvennykh imushchestv. "Zagranichnye pereselentsy v iuzhnuiu rossiiu v 1861 g." *Zhurnal ministerstva gosudarstvennykh imushchestv*, chast' 78, otdel 4 (1861): 94–96.

LL

Foreign Settlers in Southern Russia in 1861.

339.   Russia. Ministerstvo gosudarstvennykh imushchestv. "Zemle-

del'cheskaia khronika." *Zhurnal ministerstva gosudarstvennykh imushchestv*, chast' 19, otdel 5 (1846): 130–32.

LL

Agricultural Chronicle.

Announced the publication and purposes of the *Unterhaltungsblatt für deutsche Ansiedler im südlichen Russland.*

340.   Russia. Ministerstvo vnutrennikh del. "Istoricheskiia i statisticheskiia svedeniia o sareptskoi kolonii." *Zhurnal ministerstva vnutrennikh del* 28, no. 5 (1838): 245–60.

DLC

Historical and Statistical Information on the Sarepta Colony.

An official account of the religious settlement founded on the Lower Volga at Sarepta to proselytize the native peoples of that area.

341.   Russia. Ministerstvo vnutrennikh del. "Izvlechenie iz otcheta ministerstva vnutrennikh del—sostoianie kolonii." *Zhurnal ministerstva vnutrennikh del* 30, no. 12 (1838): 475–84.

DLC

Extract from the Report of the Ministry of the Interior—Condition of the Colonies.

Reports on the economic conditions in the German colonies and the inability of some to pay taxes to the government.

342.   Russia. Ministerstvo vnutrennikh del. "Kolonii saratskago okruga, v akkermanskom uezde bessarabskoi oblasti." *Zhurnal ministerstva vnutrennikh del* 42 (1853): 126–37.

NN

The Colonies of Saratskii District in the Akkerman Region of the Bessarabian Oblast.

343.   Russia. Ministerstvo vnutrennikh del. "Ob inorodcheskom, preimushchestvenno nemetskom naselenii s.-peterburgskoi gub." *Zhurnal ministerstva vnutrennikh del* 32, no. 11 (1850): 181–209.

LL

Concerning the Foreign, Primarily German, Population of St. Petersburg Province.

Contains statistical information on German colonies founded near St. Petersburg.

344.   Russia. Ministerstvo vnutrennikh del. "Ocherki puteshestviia v krym professora shmal'tsa, v 1837 godu." *Zhurnal ministerstva vnutrennikh del* 36 (1840): 422–65.

DLC

Extracts from the Travels of Professor Schmaltz in the Crimea in 1837.

German professor's notes of his travels in the Crimea, with some references to the Black Sea Germans.

345.   Russia. Ministerstvo vnutrennikh del. "Sravnitel'nyi vzgliad na sostoianie saratovskikh kolonii v 1834 i 1835 g.g." *Zhurnal ministerstva vnutrennikh del* 22, no. 10 (1836): 38–43.

DLC

A Comparative View of Conditions in the Saratov Colonies in 1834 and 1835.

346.   Russia. Ministerstvo vnutrennikh del. "Statisticheskie svedeniia o melitopol'skom uezde za 1838 g." *Zhurnal ministerstva vnutrennikh del* 31, no. 2 (1839): 295–343.

LL

Statistical Information about Melitopol District for 1838.

Several foreign colonies were in Melitopol District and are mentioned in this official account.

347.   Russia. Ministerstvo vnutrennikh del. "Statisticheskiia svedeniia ob inostrannykh poseleniiakh v rossii." *Zhurnal ministerstva vnutrennikh del* 28, no. 4 (1838): 1–83.

DLC

Statistical Information on the Foreign Settlements in Russia.

A very valuable official statistical source which includes the early German settlements in Russia.

348.   Russki [pseud.]. "O narodnom obrazovanii v nemetskikh poseleniiakh povolzh'ia." *Russkii vestnik* 250, no. 8 (August 1897): 43–64; 251, no. 9 (September 1897): 129–46; 252, no. 10 (October 1897): 183–94.

DLC NN

Public Education in the German Settlements of the Volga Region.

One of the better articles on education among the Volga Germans.

349. S., N. "Koloniia novaia studenka. Statistich. svedeniia." *Saratovskiia gubernskiia vedomosti*, no. 3 (1854): 8–9.

LL

The Colony of New Studenka: Statistical Information.

350. S. R. "Emigratsiia i pereselenie." *Vestnik novouzenskago zemstva*, no. 4 (July–August 1913): 8–42.

LL

Emigration and Migration.

Gives reasons for significant emigration of Volga Germans from Novouzensk District to America.

351. Saban'shchikov, M. "O vodvorenii kolonistov saratovskoi gubernii po kamyshinskomu uezdu." *Zavolzhskii muravei* 3, no. 17 (1832): 944–65.

LL

Concerning the Settlement of Colonists in Kamyshin District, Saratov Province.

Problems of the earliest settlements of Volga Germans.

352. Safronov, A. Ia. "O naselenii zavolzhskogo kraia, saratov. gub." *Sanktpeterburgskiia vedomosti*, no. 56 (1848): 223–24.

LL

The Population of the Trans-Volga Region in Saratov Province.

353. Safronov, A. Ia. "Statisticheskii ocherk saratovskoi gubernii." *Zhurnal ministerstva vnutrennikh del* 15, no. 7 (1846): 50–75.

LL

Statistical Sketch of Saratov Province.

354. "Saratov. Soveshchanie predstavitelei nemetskikh kolonii." *Izvestiia vserossiiskogo ts. komiteta sovetov krest'ianskikh, rabochikh, soldatskikh i kazach'ikh deputatov*, no. 93 (12 May 1918): 5.

CSt-H DLC NN

Saratov: Meeting of Representatives of the German Colonies.

Report of meeting to establish soviets and local self-government in the Volga colonies.

355. "Saratovskaia guberniia v 1846 g." *Saratovskiia gubernskiia vedomosti*, 21 (1847): 83–94; no. 22 (1847): 88–89; no. 23 (1847): 94–96; no. 25 (1847): 107–09.

LL

Saratov Province in 1846.

356. Saratovskaia uchenaia arkhivnaia komissiia. "Perechen' 'Trudov' saratovskoi uchenoi arkhivnoi komissii 1886–1902 g.g. i oglavleniia vypuskov." *Trudy saratovskoi uchenoi arkhivnoi komissii*, no. 23 (1903): i–x.

LL

A List of the Works of the Saratov Scientific Archival Committee from 1886–1902 and the Table of Contents of the Issues.

A very useful and valuable bibliography listing materials published in the *Trudy*.

357. "Saratovskiia kolonii." *Severnaia pchela*, no. 188 (1838).

LL

The Saratov Colonies.

358. "Sarepta." *Saratovskii listok*, no. 148 (1880).

LL

Sarepta.

359. "Sarepta." *Severnaia pchela*, nos. 42, 44, 45, 46, 48 (1848).

LL

Sarepta.

360. "Sarepta. Poselenie brat'ev evangelicheskoi tserkvi." *Severnaia pchela*, nos. 42, 44, 45, 46, 48 (1848).

LL

Sarepta. Settlement of the Brotherhood of the Evangelical Church.

Probably the same as entry 359.

361. Shlegel', P. "Zemskaia agronomiia i naselenie." *Sbornik sel'skokhoziaistvennykh svedenii*, no. 3 (1909): 7–13.

LL

Zemstvo Agronomy and the Populace.

Language and cultural barriers confronting *zemstvo* agronomists in their efforts to promote agriculture among the Volga Germans.

362.   Shtentsel'. "Stranichka iz proshlago (k istorii nemetskikh kolo-nii)." *Vestnik novouzenskago zemstva*, nos. 5–6 (September–December 1913): 182–93.

LL

A Page from the Past (Concerning the History of the German Colonies).

Brief history of the German colonies in Novouzensk District, Samara Province.

363.   Simbirskii, N. "Nemtsy na iuge." *Istoricheskii vestnik*, no. 12 (December 1914): 903–18.

CSt-H DLC NN

The Germans in the South.

Extremely anti-German work on settlers who were allegedly parasites living off Russia.

364.   Sokolov, S. D. "Saratovtsy pisateli i uchenye." *Trudy saratovskoi uchenoi arkhivnoi komissii*, no. 30 (1913): 257–366; no. 32 (1915): 221–84; no. 33 (1916): 135–96.

NN

Writers and Scholars of Saratov.

Biographical information on prominent men of Saratov Province, including about twenty-five Volga Germans.

365.   "Sostoianie gertsogskoi anchal't-ketenskoi kolonii (askanieva, v tavrich. obl.) v kontse 1834 g." *Zhurnal manufaktur i torgovli*, no. 4 (1835): 3–15; no. 12 (1837–1838): 550–72.

LL

The Condition of the Ducal Anhalt-Ketensk Colony (Askaniev in Tauride Province) at the End of 1834.

366.   "Sotsialisticheskoe dvizhenie sredi povolzhskikh nemtsev." *Izvestiia vserossiiskogo ts. komiteta sovetov krest'ianskikh, rabochich, soldatskikh i kazach'ikh deputatov*, no. 111 (2 June 1918): 2.

CSt-H DLC NN

The Socialist Movement among the Volga Germans.

Describes events in Volga German colonies after the November 1917 revolution.

367. "Sovdepy germanskikh kolonii." *Izvestiia vserossiiskogo ts. komiteta sovetov krest'ianskikh, rabochikh, soldatskikh, i kazach'ikh deputatov i mosk. soveta rabochikh i krasnoarmeiskikh deputatov*, no. 137 (4 July 1918): 4.

CSt-H DLC NN

Soviet Deputies of the German Colonies.

Volga German soviets reject Count Mirbach note to place colonies under protection of the German Imperial government.

368. "Sredi nemetskikh kolonistov." *Izvestiia vserossiiskogo ts. komiteta sovetov krest'ianskikh, rabochikh, soldatskikh i kazach'ikh deputatov*, no. 85 (28 April 1918): 5.

CSt-H DLC NN

Among the German Colonists.

Reports meeting of Volga German delegation with the Commissar of Nationalities, Joseph Stalin.

369. "Statisticheskie svedeniia o khersonskoi gubernii." *Khersonskiia gubernskiia vedomosti*, nos. 11, 12, 17 (1843).

LL

Statistical Information about Kherson Province.

370. "Statisticheskie svedeniia o saratovskoi gub. Iz otcheta g. nachal'nika gubernii o narodn. nravstvennosti." *Saratovskiia gubernskiia vedomosti*, no. 44 (1841): 105–06.

LL

Statistical Information about Saratov Province: From the Report of the Head of the Province Concerning the People's Morals.

371. "Statisticheskiia svedeniia o varzhavskikh koloniiakh, poselennykh v bessarabii sobstvenno tak nazyvamoi, ili budzhak." *Syn otechestva* 87, no. 33 (1823): 293–312; 88, no. 34 (1823): 19–37.

LL

Statistical Information about the Warsaw Colonies, Settled in Bessarabia Properly Called, or Budzhak.

372. "Statisticheskoe obozrenie kolonii inostrannykh poselentsev v novorossiiskom krae." *Sanktpeterburgskiia vedomosti*, no. 62 (1830): 420; no. 73 (1830): 484; no. 107 (1830): 694–95; no. 109 (1830): 708–09; no. 110 (1830): 716; no. 112 (1830): 728; no. 113 (1830): 732–33; no. 117 (1830): 757–58.

LL

Statistical Review of the Colonies of Foreign Settlers in the New Russia Territory.

373. "Svedeniia o nemetskikh poselentsakh v zakavkazskom krae." *Kavkaz*, no. 40 (1850): 159–160.

LL

Information on the German Settlers in the Transcaucasus Territory.

374. Tikheev, I. "Sarepta. Pis'mo 2-e. Istoricheskii ocherk sarepty." *Gazeta dlia sel'skikh khoziaev*, no. 59 (1862): 889–95.

LL

Sarepta. Second Letter: Historical Sketch of Sarepta.

375. Timrot, G. "Gosudarstvennaia promyshlennost' nemrespubliki." *Nizhnee povolzh'e*, no. 2 (June 1924): 62–67.

LL

State Industry in the Volga German Republic.

Development of state industry in the Volga German republic.

376. Tvalchrelidze, A. "Kolonii mennonitov vol'demfirst i aleksander-fel'd, kubanskoi oblasti." *Sbornik materialov dlia opisaniia mestnostei i plemen kavkaza* 5, no. 1 (1886): 209–74.

NN

The Mennonite Colonies of Vol'demfurst and Aleksanderfel'd in the Kuban Region.

377. Uchitel'. "O sposobakh poddershaniia distsipliny v nemetskikh shkolakh." *Vestnik novouzenskago zemstva*, no. 3 (March 1912): 49–52.

LL

Concerning the Methods of Maintaining Discipline in the German Schools.

378. Val'ter, E. "Opisanie molochanskago okruga-istoriia i nas-toiashchee polozhenie kolonii nemetskikh na molochnykh vodakh." Translated by R. Firenkrants. *Novorossiiskii kalendar' na 1851 god.* Odessa: Izdatel'stvo rishel'evskago litseia, 1852, pp. 380–97.

LL

Description of the Molochnyi District-History and Present Condition of the German Colonies on the Molochnyi Waterways.

379. Velitsyn, A. A., pseud. [Paltov, A. A.]. "Dukhovnaia zhizn' nashikh nemetskikh kolonii." *Russkii vestnik* 207, no. 3 (March 1890): 236–60; 208, no. 5 (May 1890): 212–34; 210, no. 9 (September 1890): 47–80.

CSt-H NN

The Religious Life of Our German Colonies.

Anti-German view of religious life in the German settlements. Later published as part of a monograph. See entry 171.

380. Velitsyn, A. A., pseud. [Paltov, A. A.]. "Nemetskiia kolonii na iuge." *Russkii vestnik* 207, no. 2 (February 1890): 256–99.

CSt-H DLC NN

German Colonies in the South.

Accused southern German colonists of promoting Pan-Germanism. Later published as part of a monograph. See entry 171.

381. Velitsyn, A. A., pseud. [Paltov, A. A.]. "Nemetskoe zavoevanie na iuge rossii." *Russkii vestnik* 206, no. 1 (January 1890): 142–74.

DLC NN

The German Conquest in Southern Russia.

Later published as a monograph. See entry 170.

382. Velitsyn, A. A., pseud. [Paltov, A. A.]. "Nemtsy na volge." *Russkii vestnik* 225, no. 4 (April 1893): 154–83.

CSt-H DLC NN

Germans on the Volga.

Asserts that privileges plus firm direction by the Russian government made the Volga settlers industrious and successful. Later published as part of a monograph. See entry 171.

383. Veshniakov, V. "Ekspeditsiia gosudarstvennago khoziaistva (1797–1803 g.g.)." *Russkaia starina*, no. 10 (1901): 195–205; no. 11 (1901): 403–22.

DLC NN

The Expedition of State Economy (1797–1803).

One of the many functions of this agency created by Paul I was to observe the settlement and development of foreign colonies.

384. Vitovich, A. I. "Nemetskiia kolonii na volyni." *Istoricheskii vestnik* 9 (September 1915): 884–92.

DLC NN

The German Colonies in Volynia.

A short but informative article on the German colonies in Volynia.

385. Voeikov, A. "Opisanie sarepty. Stat'ia A. Voeikova." *Severnyi arkhiv* 1 (1822): 48–69.

LL

Description of Sarepta: Article of A. Voeikov.

386. Voeikov, A. "O sostoianii kolonii iuzhnago kraia rossii v 1842 g." *Odesskii vestnik*, no. 86 (1843): 415–17.

LL

Concerning the Conditions of the Colonies of New Russia in 1842.

387. Voeikov, A. "Pis'mo iz sarepty." *Syn otechestva* 5, no. 18 (1813): 251–60.

LL

Letter from Sarepta.

388. Vuivid, G. "Spisok naselennykh mest atkarskago uezda." *Saratovskiia gubernskiia vedomosti*, nos. 11, 12, 13, 14, 15, 16 (1859).

LL

List of Populated Places in Atkarsk District.

Includes population figures on Volga colonies in Atkarsk District, Saratov Province.

389. "Vypiska iz doklada o saratovskikh koloniiakh." *Sanktpeterburgskii zhurnal*, no. 1 (1804): 92–104.

LL

Extract from a Report about the Saratov Colonies.

Part of a government report which indicated colonies had recovered from their initial economic backwardness and poverty.

390. Zaalov, M. "Mennonity i ikh kolonii na kavkaze." *Sbornik materialov dlia opisaniia mestnostei i plemen kavkaza* 23, no. 2 (1897): 89–127.

NN

The Mennonites and Their Colonies in the Caucasus.

391. "Zamechaniia na stat'iu statisticheskuiu pomeshchennuiu v No. 15 *Russkii invalid*." *Severnyi arkhiv* 25 (1827): 393–99.

LL

Remarks on the Statistical Article Published in No. 15 of *Russkii invalid*.

See entry 198.

392. "Zametki o nemetskikh koloniiakh saratovskoi gubernii." *Russkii listok*, no. 4 (1863): 75.

LL

Notes on the German Colonies of Saratov Province.

393. Zhirmunskii, V. M. "Itogi i zadachi dialektologicheskogo i etnograficheskogo izucheniia nemetskikh poselenii SSSR." *Sovetskaia etnografiia*, no. 2 (1933): 84–112.

DLC NN

Results and Tasks of Dialectical and Ethnographical Studies of the German Settlements of the Soviet Union.

Excellent summary of research done on German dialects and ethnic studies in the Russian and Soviet empires.

394. Zhirmunskii, V. M. "Problemy kolonial'noi dialektologii." *Iazyk i literatura*, no. 3 (1929): 179–220.

NN

Problems of Colonial Dialectology.

General study on dialect studies under the Soviet government.

395.   Zhirmunskii, V. M. "Vostochno-srednenemetskie govory i problema smesheniia dialektov." *Iazyk i myshlenie* 6–7 (1936):133–59.

DLC NN

Eastern-Middle-German Dialects and the Problem of the Confusion of Dialects.

Deals with dialects in Saxony, Thuringia, Silesia, and East Prussia, with only brief reference to the "kashubskii" dialect of the village of Rozental' in Melitopol District.

Newspapers

IV. Newspapers

396. *Agronomicheskiia izvestiia saratovskoi gubernii* (Saratov). Irregular; not less than four times a year.

Agricultural News of Saratov Province.

397. *Berdianskiia novosti* (Berdiansk, Tauride Province). Three times a week.

Berdiansk News.

398. *Bessarabets* (Kishinev). Daily.

The Bessarabian.

399. *Bessarabskaia zhizn'* (Kishinev). Daily.

Bessarabian Life.

400. *Bessarabskiia gubernskiia vedomosti* (Kishnev). Three times a week.

Bessarabian Provincial Gazette.

401. *Bessarabskoe sel'skoe khoziaistvo* (Kishinev). Twice a month.

Bessarabian Agriculture.

402. *Donskaia zhizn'* (Novocherkassk, Oblast of Don Fórces). Daily.

     Don Life.

403. *Donskiia oblastnyia vedomosti* (Novocherkassk, Oblast of Don Forces). Daily.

     The Don Regional Gazette.

404. *Feodosiiskii listok* (Feodosiia, Tauride Province). Twice a week.

     Feodosiia Gazette.

405. *Golos samary* (Samara). Daily.

     The Voice of Samara

406. *Khersonskaia gazeta kopeika* (Kherson). Daily

     Kherson Copeck Gazette.

407. *Khersonskiia gubernskiia vedomosti* (Kherson). Three times a week.

     Kherson Provincial Gazette.

408. *Kolonist* (Marxstadt). Irregular; 1918 only year published.

     The Colonist.

409. *Luch* (Samara). Daily.

     The Ray.

410. *Mariupol'skaia zhizn'* (Mariupol, Ekaterinoslav Province).
     Daily except Monday.

     Mariupol Life.

411. *Melitopol'skiia vedomosti* (Melitopol, Tauride Province).
     Twice a week.

     Melitopol Gazette.

412. *Nemetskii golos* (Novouzensk, Samara Province).
     Irregular; 1918 only year published.

     The German Voice.

413. *Nikolaevskaia gazeta* (Nikolaev, Kherson Province).
     Daily.

     Nikolaev Gazette.

414. *Nikolaevskaia zhizn'* (Nikolaev, Kherson Province).
     Daily.

     Nikolaev Life.

415. *Odesskaia pochta* (Odessa).
     Daily.

     The Odessa Post.

416. *Odesskii listok* (Odessa).
     Daily.

     Odessa Gazette.

417. *Odesskii vestnik* (Odessa).
     Three times a week.

     Odessa Herald.

418. *Odesskiia novosti* (Odessa).
Daily.

    Odessa News.

419. *Odesskoe obozrenie* (Odessa).
Daily.

    The Odessa Review.

420. *Odesskoe slovo* (Odessa).
Daily.

    The Odessa Word.

421. *Povolzhskaia duma* (Tsaritsyn, Saratov Province).
Weekly.

    Volga Thought.

422. *Privolzhskaia zhizn'* (Kamyshin, Saratov Province).
Twice a week.

    Volga Life.

423. *Rodnoi karai* (Kherson).
Daily.

    Native Land.

424. *Samarskii vestnik* (Samara).
Daily.

    Samara Herald.

425. *Samarskii zemledelets* (Samara).
Twice a month.

    The Samara Farmer.

426. *Samarskiia gubernskiia vedomosti* (Samara).
Twice a week.

    Samara Provincial Gazette.

427. *Saratovskaia kopechka* (Saratov).
Daily.

    The Saratov Copeck.

428. *Saratovskaia zemskaia nedelia* (Saratov).
Weekly.

    Saratov Zemstvo Weekly

429. *Saratovskii listok* (Saratov).
Daily.

    Saratov Gazette.

430. *Saratovskii vestnik* (Saratov).
Daily.

    Saratov Herald.

431. *Saratovskiia gubernskiia vedomosti* (Saratov).
Twice a week.

    The Saratov Provincial Gazette.

432. *Sbornik sel'sko-khoziaistvennykh svedenii* (Novouzensk, Samara
Province).
Monthly.

    Collection of Agricultural Information.

433. *Sel'sko-khoziaistvennyi listok kamyshinskago uezdnago zemstva*
(Kamyshin, Saratov Province).
Monthly.

    The Agricultural Gazette of the Kamyshin District Zemstvo.

434. *Tsaritsynskaia mysl'* (Tsaritsyn, Saratov Province). Daily.

    Tsaritsyn Thought.

435. *Tsaritsynskii vestnik* (Tsaritsyn, Saratov Province). Daily.

    Tsaritsyn Herald.

436. *Vedomosti odesskago gradonachal'stva* (Odessa). Daily.

    Gazette of the Town of Odessa.

437. *Volga* (Saratov). Daily.

    Volga.

438. *Volzhskoe slovo* (Samara). Daily.

    Volga Word.

Subject Index

Subject Index

Numbers refer to entries

A

Agriculture, 105, 323, 332; education, 339, 361; equipment, 320; grain harvests, 234; grain trade, 114–16; land tenure, 93, 99; livestock raising, 164, 324; peasant farming, 149; production, 128; planting methods, 40, 72–73, 255, 327, 336; regulations, 42; tobaccco growing, 328, 335; viniculture, 254

Aleksanderfel'd, 376

Alexandertal, 239

Anhalt–Ketensk, 365

Anti–German literature, 85, 151, 160, 172, 193, 205, 304, 379; directed against Black Sea Germans, 65, 80–81, 108, 155, 170–71, 363, 380–81: directed against Volga Germans, 171, 192, 260, 382

Askaniev. See Anhalt–Ketensk

Atkarsk District, 388

B

Banking and credit, 92, 219

Baronsk. See Katharinenstadt

Bessarabia, 14, 19, 107; geography of, 107; German colonies in, 16, 157, 332, 342, 371

Bibliographies, 1–13, 356

Biography, 161, 364

Black Sea Germans, 29–30, 158, 265, 281–82, 344, 378; administration of, 106 213, 295; colonization by, 17, 155, 157, 203, 249–50, 254, 318, 331; donations to war effort by 321; economy of, 305, 320, 322, 341, 346, 365, 386; farming methods of, 255, 327, 336; intercolony assistance of, 330; land tenure of, 68, 93, 227; livestock raising of, 324; organization of, 23; postrevolution conditions of, 306; publications for, 339; statistical information on, 140, 143, 319, 334, 338, 347, 372; *zemstvos* of, 83. See also Anti–German literature

C

Caucasus colonies, 178, 287, 307, 329, 373, 390

Customary law, 2

D

Department of State Economy, 383

Derzhavin, Gavriil Romanovich, 62

Description and·travel, 36, 58, 77, 344

Deutsch–Shcherbakovka, 263

127

Z

Author Index

Author Index

James Long is Associate Professor of History and a staff member of the Germans from Russia in Colorado Study Project at Colorado State University, Fort Collins. He earned his doctorate at the University of Wisconsin with a major in Russian and Soviet Studies. He has published earlier research and reviews in journals in this country and abroad.

This work grew from Dr. Long's study of Soviet library and archival materials during a six-month stay in the USSR in 1976 as a research scholar under the cultural exchange program between the United States and the Soviet Union.